the COURAGE *to be* PROFITABLE

the COURAGE *to be* PROFITABLE

GET AND STAY

PROFITABLE

IN LESS THAN

30 MINUTES

A MONTH

RUTH KING

NEW YORK

the COURAGE *to be* PROFITABLE
Get and Stay Profitable in Less than 30 Minutes a Month

ISBN 978-1-61448-462-2 paperback
ISBN 978-1-61448-463-9 eBook
Library of Congress Control Number:

Morgan James Publishing
The Entrepreneurial Publisher
5 Penn Plaza, 23rd Floor
New York City, New York 10001
(212) 655-5470 office • (516) 908-4496 fax
www.MorganJamesPublishing.com

Cover Design by:
Rachel Lopez
www.r2cdesign.com

Interior Design by:
Bonnie Bushman
bonnie@caboodlegraphics.com

In an effort to support local communities, raise awareness and funds, Morgan James Publishing donates a percentage of all book sales for the life of each book to Habitat for Humanity Peninsula and Greater Williamsburg.

Get involved today, visit
www.MorganJamesBuilds.com.

Dedication

THIS BOOK IS DEDICATED to entrepreneurs worldwide who have had the courage to start or buy a business. May you have the courage to get and stay profitable.

Table of Contents

Figures

Read This First

The Tale of Two Business Owners

THROUGHOUT THIS BOOK, you will hear some of my clients' stories. The names and certain aspects of the stories not affecting the outcome have been changed to protect confidentiality. Here are the first two stories:

COMPANY A

Steve took over a business from his father. He was hugely successful, grew the business from under $1,000,000 to over $10,000,000, and earned millions of dollars. He looked at financial statements every month, which showed a profit. Life was good.

The company had several departments. The market for the department where the company generated the majority of the revenues and profits was rapidly declining. A smaller department was growing. His advisory board (I wasn't on it) suggested starting another department in a different but allied market segment that he knew nothing about. He invested hundreds of thousands of dollars to start this business segment.

Steve intellectually acknowledged that his largest department was in decline, but he refused to do anything about it. He didn't want to lay off employees who had been with the company for fifteen or more years. My encouragement to grow the smaller, profitable department and stop the department that was bleeding cash fell on deaf ears.

The unprofitable department got smaller. The losses grew each month. The new department was never profitable. These departments were sucking the cash out of the company. Steve saw the decline on the financials. Instead of growing the smaller department, he put more wasted effort and dollars into the new department. Steve took some people from the declining department and put them in this department. They didn't know what they were doing, and he didn't have the appropriate accounting set up to show that they weren't doing their jobs and were not generating profits.

The warning signs were there for three years. Steve absolutely refused to shut down the first department, even though he knew it could bankrupt the company. Finally, after three years of prodding, he got the courage to fire the employees, go to his few customers in the first department and tell them that he wasn't going to provide products and services to them, and find people who could handle the new department. It was too little, too late. The hugely successful company that had grown to more than $10 million in sales was no longer. What was left was gobbled up by a former competitor. Steve didn't have the courage to take action when the warning signs were there for three years.

COMPANY B

George took over the family business from his father and his uncle. His father and uncle grew the company to a multimillion dollar business without really knowing the bottom line of their company. Financials? Never looked at them. Pricing? They had no idea what their costs really were and priced according to when their "gut" said "enough." Their "gut" was wrong!

When George bought out his father and uncle, he didn't understand a balance sheet or a profit and loss statement. But he did know about cash, and he didn't think there was enough to keep the company afloat. Creditors were calling, and they were on COD with many of their vendors.

The company was in a cash-flow crisis. George was smart enough to know that he needed help fast. He courageously took action and brought in people who could help him.

George quickly learned about profit and loss statements, balance sheets, and what they meant. The pricing changed to profitable pricing. His salespeople learned how to sell profitably at higher dollar amounts.

Some people didn't conform to the changes and were fired. Others left. George was focused and communicated with everyone the reasons for the changes. Yes, they were difficult. Yes, firing non-productive people was hard. The result? His profits increased, and he slowly grew the company's cash position and bottom-line profits.

What was the difference between Steve and George? The courage to look at the financial statements, spot the issues, and take action before the problems became major crises. George had the courage to do something immediately, even though he didn't understand financial statements. Steve understood financial statements, but he didn't act on what they were telling him.

The Courage to Be Profitable can help you understand the financial part of your company. If you are like George, you'll take the information in this book, apply it to your business, implement necessary changes, and create a profitable business—in just thirty minutes a month.

However, if you are like Steve, and you don't react quickly to what your financial statements are telling you, then this book can't help you. You don't have the courage to be profitable.

The choice is yours.

Introduction

"I HAVE TO LOOK at a financial statement? No way. That's Greek to me."

If you are not willing to look at a financial statement, you should put this book down and close your business today! Why? You are like a frog in a pot of water. When you put a frog in a pot of cold water and slowly increase the heat, the frog is cooked before he can jump out and save himself. He can't see minor issues before they become major problems. If you don't look at your financial statements or they are inaccurate, you can't see the warning signs that, if you don't take care of, can put you out of business.

You are like a cooked frog: soon you're dead without realizing it.

You probably are like most business owners. You started your business to help people by producing a great product or service. You're really good at producing that product or service, and your business grows. More sales come in the door. However, are those sales profitable? The only way you know is by producing accurate financial statements each month. Unless you are an accountant or bookkeeper, you've got to learn this part of your business.

This is where most small business owners struggle. They don't understand their financial statements and don't even think about them in the beginning stages of the business. Their accountant produces their tax returns each year. Sometimes there is a big surprise—a tax bill and no cash to pay it. Where did it go? You'll find out in *The Courage to Be Profitable*.

Do you have the courage to run a profitable business? Before you immediately think "yes," realize what this includes:

- Selling to and retaining a profitable customer base
- Producing high-quality, profitable products and services
- Monitoring cash flow (not cash—cash flow)
- Understanding and reacting to timely, accurate financial statements

The word "profitable" appears a lot: your business revolves around profit in all areas of your company. If your customers cost you more than they generate in sales, you don't need those customers. The only way to find out if you have profitable customers is to track their revenues, costs, and when they pay their bills.

Are your products and services profitable? You don't know unless you get a financial statement each month, look at it, analyze it, and take action based on what you find.

What is your cash flow pattern? You must know how many days it takes, on average, from the time you send a bill to a client until you receive payment.

There are three stages to ongoing profitability:

- Stage One: Understand the financial part of your business
- Stage Two: Implement the financial review and trend analysis each month
- Stage Three: React to and take action based on what your financial statements are telling you

Do you have the courage to be profitable? Will you get your financial statements each month, analyze them, understand them, face the good and the bad, and do something about them?

Or will you "hide under the blanket" and do nothing—even though you know something just isn't right with your business?

Have the courage to face your financial statements each month. When they are accurate, you celebrate the profits, watch your cash flow, look at the trends, and ensure that you stay profitable. You have the courage to spot the minor issues and do something about them before they become major crises—and your business becomes another business failure statistic.

"It's easy to understand financial statements." *Yeah, right,* you sarcastically think.

Actually you've probably done harder things. Think about the first time you took up a new sport, such as tennis or golf. The first time you played you were probably terrible at it. However, you liked it, and you kept on trying. Eventually you got comfortable with it, got better and better at it, and enjoyed the sport.

Or you spent thousands of hours in school learning a trade. It was hard in the beginning. However, you kept at it because you enjoyed it and wanted to make a career out of it.

Financial statements are actually easy. They were developed about one thousand years ago by the Venetian monks who had to keep track of the rich Italians' money. They *had* to make it simple.

There were no adding machines, calculators, or computers. We have it so much easier today! You'll discover that financial statements are no more than addition and subtraction. You can use a calculator and a computer software program to help you.

Yes, you'll learn a few new terms. But you learned more terms and vocabulary to have the knowledge to produce your products and services.

If your experience is similar to that of most of my clients, the first few months of financial reviews are harder because you have to "look up" the analysis terms. However, each month's review becomes faster and easier. Within six months the analysis is quick, and you start wondering why you ever thought financial statement reviews were hard.

If you have the courage to be profitable, you have the courage to learn a few simple formats and terms to find out if you have enough cash, are building inventory, have a collection problem, are profitable, and much more each month. You'll invest only about thirty minutes to make sure your business is heading in the direction you want it to go. *The Courage to Be Profitable* shows you how.

Stage One

UNDERSTAND THE FINANCIAL PART OF YOUR BUSINESS

||||||||||||||||||||||||||||||||||||||||||||||||||||||||||||||||||||||||||||||||||||||||||||||||

Chapter 1

Do You Have a
Hobby or a Business?

||||||||||||||||||||||||||||||||||||||||||||||||||||||||||||||||||||||||||||||||||||||||||||||||

If you don't pay attention to your financial statements, you have a hobby. Hobbyists love what they do, operate their businesses for fun, and don't care whether they make a profit or not. They are doing it for enjoyment only and never pay attention to whether what they are doing is profitable.

Hobbyists are doing what I call "working for wages." They spend hours at their businesses, usually working fifty hours per week or more. They may have employees. They never look at their pricing and don't make the time to review their financial statements. At the end of the year, they may or may not have made a profit. They really don't care.

When they get tired, hurt, or can no longer work at their business for whatever reason, they have nothing to show for their years of effort. There are few assets worth selling. There is no cash. There may be a customer list. However, those customers are used to paying the lowest prices. If a company buys the hobbyist's customer list, those customers usually leave that new company because they get "sticker shock" at the prices that new company needs to charge to earn a profit.

Business owners also love what they do. However, they put a value on what they do to ensure that their efforts are profitable. They may work sixty or more hours per week. However, those are profitable hours that lead to a profitable bottom line.

They invest the thirty minutes each month to review their financial statements. They understand what they mean. They look at the business trends. They make good business decisions based on what the statements are telling them each month. Business owners can spot the minor issues and take care of those issues before they become major crises.

If you want a business with profits, then have the courage to learn about financial statements and grow your business profitably so there is something left after years of hard, enjoyable work.

Are you a hobbyist, or do you have the courage to be profitable?

at what he actually earned. His $50,000 net profit didn't look so good to him anymore.

John asked me what to do about it. I reminded him that making a profit was good. The next step was to decide the net profit per hour that he wants to earn in the current fiscal year and do what is necessary to make it happen. Only John could decide what net profit per hour he wants to earn.

My philosophy: If your net profit per hour is less than you could earn at a fast-food restaurant, why are you putting yourself through all the stress of operating a business? Or is your business just a hobby?

Chapter 3

Cash-Basis Accounting Gives You a False Sense of Security

Many CPAs report company taxes on a cash basis. Sometimes there are tax advantages for doing so. However, your operating financial statements, the statements you use to guide your daily business operations, should be set up on an accrual basis.

Here's the story of Jane, whose experience shows why you must operate on an accrual basis.

> Jane's CPA reported her taxes on a cash basis, so she thought that she should set up her books the same way. She opted for cash basis when she set up her QuickBooks® accounting system. She didn't understand the difference.
>
> After she got help, Jane learned that in cash accounting a sale was recorded when the company got the money for the

sale, rather than when the company invoiced the customer. The system recorded an expense when the company paid vendors, rather than when the vendor invoices were received. Even though there were accounts payable and accounts receivable in QuickBooks®, they were never reported on her cash-basis financial statements.

Jane never looked at her balance sheet. She only printed out the profit and loss statement. She never saw that the company didn't report accounts payable, accounts receivable, or inventory, since they were on the balance sheet. As long as the bills got paid, and the profit and loss statement showed that the company was profitable most of the time, Jane didn't worry about it.

Some months, when the company was very busy, the profit and loss statement showed a loss. Other months, when the company had less sales, the profit and loss statement showed a profit on the bottom line. This didn't make much sense to Jane. How could the company be busy and not be profitable?

Over a period of time, the company's financial statements began to bother Jane a lot. What she was seeing from operations didn't match what she saw on the financial statements. There were always more bills than cash to pay them. Jane discovered that her company was living under a false sense of security.

After switching the company's accounting from cash basis to accrual basis, Jane was shocked to find out that her company was actually not profitable!

How could this be? In cash-basis accounting, the only time an expense is recorded is when the bill is paid. So the *company was almost always profitable because they didn't pay their bills unless they had the cash to pay them! In the months where there was a lot of cash to pay bills that had accumulated, the company could show a loss (more expenses than receipts).*

In accrual-based accounting, an expense is recorded even if the bill isn't paid. Jane saw that when the revenues and expenses were recorded at the time they were incurred, she could easily make sure that all expenses for the projects were deducted from the revenues for that project. She discovered that the company performed work that wasn't profitable!

Jane's accountant told her that, for her company, it was better to report taxes on a cash basis. However, she could operate her business on an accrual basis. It was up to her.

Operate your company's accounting on an accrual basis. Your financial statements show your accounts payable, accounts receivable, and inventory levels. You'll know each month, assuming your information is accurate, whether your company is really profitable.

Chapter 4

Profits Are Not Cash: You Can Be Profitable and Go Out of Business

The value at the bottom of your profit and loss statement is not cash. It is a positive number when your revenues exceed your expenses. It is a negative number when your expenses exceed your revenue.

It is a profit or a loss. It is not the amount of cash you have in your bank account.

Profits are turned into cash when you collect for your products and services, and you pay the expenses to produce those products and services. Hopefully there is cash at the end of this process!

There may be months when your company shows a profit and doesn't have enough cash to pay its bills. There may be other months when your company shows a loss and has plenty of cash in the bank. You can be profitable and have no cash. You can have a loss and have cash. However, if you have a loss for a long period of time, your cash will dwindle. You must have profitable sales to have a chance of generating positive cash flow.

Many times companies show a great profit and have little cash in their bank accounts. When it is time to report the profit to the Internal Revenue Service, the company doesn't have the cash to pay the taxes on the profits.

Where are those profits? In accounts receivable, in inventory, and invested in the personnel and equipment it must have to produce growing revenues.

How can a company be profitable and go out of business? Here's Peter's story:

> *Peter operated a very successful contracting company. It showed profits for more than ten years, and the company grew to become a multimillion-dollar company. Three of his largest customers filed bankruptcy the same week. This left him with over $1,000,000 of uncollectable receivables. He didn't have the cash to survive. So, a very profitable business went out of business.*

Make sure you have enough cash on hand to cover operations for a three-to-six-month period of time.

Have the courage to call your customers when payment terms are thirty days and the company hasn't received payment on that thirty-first day. Or, if someone at your company handles collections, review the accounts receivable weekly and ensure that person calls on the thirty-first day. Your survival depends on it!

Chapter 5

What Is Cash?

The best way to describe cash and cash flow is to look at Figure 1.

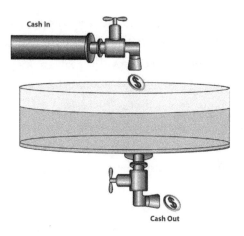

Figure 1. Cash Flow Diagram

Think about a tank that is filled with water. The level of the tank rises and falls depending on whether you are adding water to the tank through a spigot, or decreasing water from the tank through a drain.

Now, imagine that the water in the tank is the number of dollars in your checking account. The level of water (i.e., your cash) increases when you open the spigot and add to it through *collections* on sales (notice I didn't say *sales*), personal or investor loans to the company, interest on investments, tapping your line of credit, or selling assets.

Note: These are the major additions to cash. There are some other, uncommon additions, such as lawsuit payments, that are not included in your operations cash flow.

The level of water decreases when you open the drain to pay for inventory, payroll, rent, utilities, and other direct and overhead expenses.

Every time you add cash to the tank through collections on sales, etc., the level of cash in the tank rises. Every time you write a check, the level in the tank drops. The goal is to keep the level of water in the tank high enough to ensure you have sufficient cash to operate your business on a day-to-day basis.

The drain must be shut before there is no more water in the tank. If you run out of water (i.e., cash), you are out of business.

Sales don't count in cash flow. Collections of those sales count in cash flow.

Profits or losses don't count in cash flow. What happens when you turn those profits and losses into cash counts in cash flow.

Chapter 6

What Is a Balance Sheet?

A balance sheet is simply a snapshot of the health of your business at a point in time. So many business owners have told me, "I never look at my balance sheet." When I ask why, usually the answer is, "It doesn't tell me anything." (My interpretation of that is that they don't understand it.) The reality is that balance sheets tell you a lot about what's going on in your business.

In my opinion, they are more important than profit and loss statements. Why? Your balance sheet answers the question, "How is my company doing?" from an overall perspective. It tells you:

- If you can pay your bills
- If you are taking on too much debt
- If you have a collection problem
- If you have productive employees

- If you have an inventory problem (if your business has inventory)

Your balance sheet is literally a snapshot for one moment in time. The reason it is a snapshot is because your balance sheet is constantly changing. It is constantly changing because your cash is constantly changing. You have a different cash balance every day, which means that your balance sheet changes every day.

Calculate your balance sheet at consistent moments in time. The best times are usually the last day of each month and the last day of your fiscal year. Every month and every year are good time frames to compare so you can answer the question, "How is my company doing?"

The balance sheet is called the balance sheet because assets must balance liabilities plus net worth. Figure 2 shows the balance sheet format with the major categories.

Assets are things of value. Liabilities are things that you owe. Net worth is what I call your "fudge factor"—i.e., if you had to close your doors tomorrow and convert all of your assets to cash and pay off all of your liabilities, your business's net worth is what would be left.

Let's take each of the major components of the balance sheet.

ASSETS

There are two types of assets: current assets and long-term assets (also called fixed assets). Let's look at current assets first.

Current Assets

Current assets are either cash or things that can be turned into cash within a year. The major categories of current assets are cash,

ASSETS	LIABILITIES
Current Assets	Current Liabilities
Cash	Accounts payable
Investments	Line of credit
Accounts receivable	Deferred income-svc agr.
Inventory	Warranty
Prepaid expenses	Taxes payable
Total Current Assets	Current portion of long term debt
	Total Current Liabilities
Long term (fixed) Assets	
Furniture	Long Term Liabilities
Tools	Notes payable
Office equipment	Owner payable
Vehicles	Total Long Term Liabilities
Buildings	
Deposits	TOTAL LIABILITIES
Less accumulated depreciation	
Total Long Term Assets	

	NET WORTH
	Capital Stock
	Retained Earnings
	TOTAL NET WORTH
TOTAL ASSETS	**TOTAL LIABILITIES & NET WORTH**

Figure 2. Balance Sheet Format

investments, accounts receivable, inventory, and prepaid expenses. Occasionally you'll have some other current assets. However, on an operational or day-to-day basis, you'll generally have these categories.

Cash is cash. Cash includes the money in your bank account, petty cash in your office, and money-market funds that can easily be converted to cash.

Investments are stocks and other relatively liquid investments that can be sold quickly for cash. Look at the cash portion of your business as what you use to write a check immediately to pay an invoice.

There are three types of **accounts receivable**. The first is *trade receivables,* or the amount customers owe you for work performed. The second is *employee receivables,* or the amount employees have borrowed from the company. The third is *owner receivables,* or the amount owners or officers have borrowed from the company. If owners plan on paying the company back within a year, then include owner receivables in current assets. If owners don't expect to pay the money back within a year, then put owner receivables in long-term assets.

Many times you'll also see an allowance for *doubtful accounts.* If an invoice is 120 days old or older, this invoice amount may be put into an allowance for doubtful accounts. The likelihood is that it's going to be tough to collect that money, and you may not get it. So, many companies don't count it in the day-to-day receivables that are usually collected in 30 to 45 days.

The next major current asset category is **inventory**. Many service companies—i.e., companies that do not produce physical goods—do not have inventory. So if your company has inventory, read on!

One of my favorite sayings is "Inventory is a bet." You have to be very careful with inventory. Unless you are ordering materials specifically for a project, you are betting your hard-earned dollars that you will be able to sell a part when you buy it from a vendor. So when your employee purchases two widgets when you need one for a customer, that's a bet. Your employee is betting, with your money, that he'll be able to sell that second widget before he forgets that it's in your warehouse.

Your balance sheet helps you track your bets. I have been to a lot of offices and warehouses and seen bets on shelves. Five, six, seven, and ten years of inventory just sitting on a shelf, gathering dust. You've paid for it, you bet, and you lost.

Count inventory yearly and account for it each month. I've seen a lot of balance sheets that have the same inventory value each month. That's not real. If your company has inventory, you purchase material and use material every business day. It is very unlikely that you will have the same dollar volume of inventory at the beginning and the end of the month. Start with a beginning inventory, add the purchases, and subtract the usage. Most accounting programs let you do this easily as long as you track job cost.

The last major current asset category is **prepaid expenses.** Prepaid expenses are those expenses that you paid that cover a longer period of time than one month. For example, if you pay your insurance bill once a year and it covers the entire year, the only expense you have every month is one-twelfth of that total insurance payment. If you paid the entire yearly premium of $1,200 in January, you have $100 in insurance expenses in January and $1,100 in prepaid expenses. In February, you'll have another $100 in insurance expenses and $1,000 in prepaid expenses. This continues for the year until all of the insurance expense is paid, and there are no prepaid insurance expenses on the balance sheet.

Here's why the insurance payment is an asset to you: If you decide to change your insurance company in the middle of the year, the first insurance company has to refund you the portion of the year that hasn't been insured. You'll get the cash back, so that's a prepaid expense. There are other expenses that you might pay in advance for a quarter, six months, or one year. These are normally prepaid expenses. The expense is an asset to you until you use it.

There are two other categories of current assets used by contractors and manufacturing companies: **work-in-progress** and **over/underbillings**. Work-in-progress is used when you accrue revenues and expenses until the contracts are completed. Underbillings occur when you have completed more work on a project than you've billed to date. Overbillings are when you bill more than the percentage of work completed on a project.

Long-Term (Fixed) Assets

Long-term assets, or fixed assets, are what I call "the stuff." They are furniture, computers, buildings, vehicles, and things in your company that don't turn into cash easily. They are the things that you see on a day-to-day basis that you use for a long period of time. These are assets that do not turn into cash within a year.

The tax laws constantly change with the amount of purchases that you can "write off" each year. That means you can expense these purchases rather than having to depreciate them over a longer time period. For example, if you purchase a filing cabinet, you might consider that an expense and not an asset. Talk with your accountant to see what is appropriate for your company.

Another long-term asset is a deposit. Many times when you move into a new facility, the landlord asks for a rent deposit, or the utility company asks for a deposit. These deposits are held for a specific period of time, which is usually longer than one year.

Remember to put an owner receivable in long-term assets if owners aren't planning to repay the loan within a year. As an owner, it is your prerogative to make a company loan to yourself. However, if you don't plan to repay that loan within a year, it belongs in fixed assets.

Be real and be accurate with your company's balance sheet. Garbage in equals garbage out. You can't make intelligent decisions about the future of your company with inaccurate financial statements.

LIABILITIES

Liabilities are debts that your business owes. Like assets, liabilities are divided into two segments: current liabilities and long-term liabilities.

Current Liabilities

Current liabilities are debts that must be paid within one year. The major categories of current liabilities are **accounts payable, accrued taxes** (payroll taxes, income taxes, state taxes, local taxes, etc.), **deferred income, warranty,** and **current portion of long-term debt**.

There are three types of **accounts payable.** The first is trade payables, or the amount your company owes to suppliers. The second is employee payables, which occur when an employee loans money to the company. The third is owner payables, which occur when an owner loans the company money. If you expect the company to pay an employee or owner a loan back within a year, the loan amount goes into current liabilities. If you don't expect the company to repay that loan in a year, the loan amount goes in long-term liabilities.

The next major category of current liabilities is **accrued taxes.** Generally these taxes are payroll taxes, federal and state income taxes, sales taxes, franchise taxes, and a number of geographically local taxes. These are all due within one year, and usually a lot sooner than that. Please verify that payroll taxes are current.

Business owners are personally liable for payroll tax payments. Make sure that you see the payment confirmation numbers. Interest and penalties on these taxes are expensive!

The next current liabilities category is **deferred income.** There are two major types of deferred income: service contracts and deposits (different from asset deposits). Many companies sell service contracts that cover a year or longer. Therefore the company is liable to perform that service for the year or longer time period.

When your company receives money for a service contract before the work is completed, the company has a liability to perform that work. This is deferred income. When the work gets performed, the liability goes away and the company earns revenue.

When your company wins a project and doesn't plan to start work for an extended period of time (i.e., three months, etc.), you may ask for a deposit as a down payment. That deposit, even though it is cash, is a liability, because you must refund the money if your company does not do the project. Very similar to the service contracts, the company has a liability until it performs the work. So customer deposits for future work are current liabilities until the work is performed.

The next major category of current liabilities is **warranty.** This account can become substantial for companies. As a condition for performing a project, the company has to warranty the work for a period of time, usually one year. This is different from deferred income, because warranty is not part of revenues. It is calculated as part of job cost. Therefore each project cost should include warranty expense. Since the company hasn't performed the warranty at the conclusion of the job, this obligation is recorded in current liabilities under the warranty category. It becomes a liability to your company until the warranty period is up. At the end of the warranty period, any unused expense is considered additional profit to the project.

If your company has a warranty problem, the expense for taking care of that problem comes out of the warranty fund. That's why it's there. Hopefully, there are enough funds to take care of any warranty issues.

The next major current liabilities category is **current portion of long-term debt**. This occurs when your company purchases a vehicle, computer system, or other fixed asset and takes out a loan longer than one year to pay for that asset. Let's assume you obtain a three-year vehicle loan from the bank. Of the three-year period, one year's principal repayment is due within a year. This is the current portion of long-term debt. The other two years go into long-term liabilities. Once twelve months of payments have been made, there is one year in long-term liabilities and one year in current portion of long-term debt. Once the second twelve months of payments are made, there is only one year left in current liabilities and no long-term liability for that vehicle.

In summary, current liabilities are debts that must be repaid within one year. Let's look at the other liability segment: long-term liabilities.

Long-Term Liabilities

Long-term liabilities are debts that are repaid in longer than one year. Generally these are **notes payable** and **owner's payables**.

There are several types of **notes.** They include vehicle notes, mortgages, and notes to owners. Only one year's payments go into current liabilities. The rest of the principal payment amount goes into long-term liabilities.

If an owner loans the company money that will be repaid in longer than one year, this loan also goes into long-term liabilities.

NET WORTH

The final segment of the balance sheet is *net worth*. Net worth is also called stockholder's equity, capital, or a number of other terms depending on the legal form of your business (sole proprietor, LLC, corporation, etc.) This value is what is left if your company had to liquidate all of its assets to pay its liabilities. There are two major categories in net worth: **stockholder's or owner's equity** and **retained earnings**.

Stockholder's equity is the value that stockholders have invested in a corporation. *Owner's equity* is the value that the owner of a company invests in his business, if it isn't incorporated. This investment can be made during the start of the business or as additional investments during operation of the business. Many times owners sell stock to employees or other investors. This stock value goes in the net-worth segment.

Retained earnings are that portion of a corporation's profits that your company didn't distribute as dividends at the end of its fiscal year. Most small businesses don't take dividends. If they take a distribution, they take it as a bonus. (The bonus is expensed on the profit and loss statement before profits are calculated.) Retained earnings grow from year to year, as long as the company is profitable. For an unprofitable year, retained earnings shrink. As company profits increase, then the net worth of the business increases. As profits decrease, the net worth of the business decreases.

In summary, the balance sheet is a snapshot of the health of your business at one moment in time. It tells you if you have enough cash to pay your bills, if you have too much inventory or debt, and if you have a collection problem. It tracks your assets, your liabilities, and your net worth. Tracking these numbers is important to ensure that the business remains viable.

Chapter 7

What Is a Profit and Loss Statement?

Profit and loss statements are also called income statements. Most accountants call them profit and loss statements. Most people who come from the finance world (like I did) call them income statements. An income statement is a picture of the profit and loss of your company over a period of time. It's a cumulative statement. Unlike the balance sheet, which is a snapshot of the health of your business at a moment in time, a profit and loss (P&L) statement looks at how the company has performed over a period of time. At the end of that period of time, usually one month or one year, the profit and loss statement "starts over."

Most accounting programs provide for options with respect to the company's profit and loss statements. Generally owners choose to see month to date and year to date. Other options are month to date this year and month to date last year, as well as year to date this year and year to date last year

Many companies departmentalize their profit and loss statements. This means that each department has its own operating statement. This way you can truly tell which segments of your business are profitable.

The profit and loss statement format is shown in Figure 3.

P and L Format

Sales
- Cost of goods sold (COGS)
= Gross profit

Gross profit
- General and administrative expenses (G&A)
= Net operating profits or net profit before taxes (PBT)

Net operating profits
- Other Expense + Other Income
= Profit before taxes

Profit before taxes
- Taxes
= Net Profit

Figure 3. Profit and Loss Statement Format

The profit and loss equation starts with **sales or revenues**. Subtract the cost of sales from sales. The result is gross profit. Then subtract overhead from gross profit, and the result is net operating profit. Then subtract other expense or add other income, and the result is profit before taxes. Finally, subtract taxes. The result is net profit.

There are different categories of sales and numerous methods to departmentalize (break apart) revenues. The important thing is to ensure that each department stands alone and gets its own profit and loss statement. Departmentalization is covered in chapter 8. Each department should be profitable. If it isn't, fix it or eliminate that department!

The next category is **cost of goods sold,** also known as **cost of sales,** or **direct costs.** These are expenses that are incurred because something was sold. Typical direct costs include direct materials, direct labor, subcontracts, commissions, warranty, permits, and freight.

There are also some gray areas. Some companies include labor burden and truck costs (for employees performing work outside of the office) in costs of goods sold. Their reasoning is that there is a burden associated with each hour of direct labor (FICA and Medicare expenses, unemployment taxes, health insurance, worker's compensation, union dues, etc.), and these expenses would not be incurred if the employee didn't have an hour of labor. With respect to truck costs, the thinking is, "If I didn't have to perform work at customers' homes or offices, I wouldn't have truck cost. Each employee has a truck, and without a truck, the employee can't do his job."

Some owners account for truck costs in overhead. There is no right or wrong answer. Put these expenses where you are comfortable with putting these expenses. You must be consistent. That means if in one month you put burden in direct cost, the next month you can't put it in overhead cost.

Gross profit is the result of subtracting cost of goods sold (COGS), or direct expenses, from sales.

To get **net operating profit,** subtract overhead from gross profit.

Overhead is the expense that your business incurs so that it can stay in business. Typical overhead includes rent, telephone, and utilities. You must pay these bills each month irrespective of the sales you generate. Even if you had zero sales, you would still have to pay your utility bill.

Some companies divide overhead into two pieces: compensation expenses and general and administrative (G&A) expenses. G&A expenses are also called operational expenses.

Compensation expenses are salary-related expenses. They include office salaries, owner salaries, unapplied time, and labor burden—if labor burden is included here rather than in direct expenses. In either case, your compensation expenses will have the labor burden for the office personnel's and owner's salaries.

The only costs that go into direct costs are those costs that are incurred when an employee generates revenues or sales for the company. Meeting time, training time, travel time, or any time that is not generating revenue and is paid for by the company but can't be charged to a customer is unapplied time and goes into overhead.

One owner asked me why I choose to break out compensation overhead from G&A overhead. One of the most critical areas to track is labor. Good labor productivity usually means profitable sales. Most companies can't afford to have an employee put eight hours on his time sheet and work on customers' projects for only four of those eight hours. The best way to closely watch labor expense is to put it in its own special category in overhead. This way every month, when you review the financial statements, you can see how much was spent on all types of labor. If it is out of line, you can do something immediately.

Here's Chuck's story:

> *Chuck didn't believe he had labor-productivity problems. The only part of his P&L statement he looked at was the net profit before taxes. The reality was that field employees were putting 40 hours on their time sheets but only producing revenues for 25 to 30 hours per week. I asked the bookkeeper to change the place where the "unapplied time" was printed on the profit and loss statement. Instead of having unapplied time buried in the list of overhead expenses, I had her move this expense line right before total expenses and operating profit. Chuck saw these numbers every month when he looked at the net profit. He couldn't miss the unapplied time, because it was the last expense before net operating profit! Very soon unapplied time decreased dramatically, which increased the profitability of the company.*

So if you think there is a problem with either direct or indirect expenses, you can change where those categories appear on your P&L. It's your statement. You can look at it whichever way you'd like to look at it.

The next segment of the profit and loss statement is G&A overhead, or operational overhead. These expenses include rent, utilities, dues and subscriptions, accounting fees, bank charges, donations, telephone, insurance, travel, entertainment, and many other expenses the business incurs that are not a result of selling something. If vehicle costs are not included in direct labor, they go here.

Operational overhead expenses are the expenses that don't change radically on a month-by-month basis. Look at this section of the profit and loss statement for consistency.

For example, if the company's rent is $1,000 a month, and there is a rent expense in January and not one in February, you know that your P&L is wrong. Your landlord requires that you pay your rent each month. Find out why there was not a rent expense in February.

Likewise, watch insurance expenses. If the insurance payments are due once per year, the month they are due should not show the entire insurance expense. The yearly insurance expense paid up front is an asset, a prepaid expense. Each month one-twelfth of the payment is considered an expense to the business.

Overhead expenses are subtracted from gross profit to arrive at net operating profit. This is the "ordinary profit," the profit that is generated from regular sales and expenses that occur on a day-to-day basis.

Sometimes there is income or expense that is not generated from day-to-day operations. This gets added or subtracted next. **Other income** is usually interest received from investments or gain on sales of assets. If the company sells a fixed asset such as a vehicle, it might have a gain on the sale of that vehicle. It happens when, on the balance sheet, the value of the vehicle is $1,000 and the company sells it for $2,000. The extra $1,000 is other income to the company. Yes, you have to pay taxes on that income.

Other expenses are usually losses on sales of assets. If the company sells that vehicle for $500, and its value on the balance sheet is $1,000, the company has a loss of $500 that it can deduct from profits.

Other income and expenses are non-operating revenue or expenses that the company receives. This part of the income statement handles extraordinary events—i.e., unusual income and unusual expenses. They are not the day-to-day operating income and expenses.

After adding other income and subtracting other expenses, the company has **profit before taxes.** Then income taxes are subtracted to arrive at net income. This is the figure that is added to retained earnings on the balance sheet.

The profit and loss statement formula is straightforward. It is sales minus cost of goods sold equals gross profit. Subtract overhead from gross profit to arrive at net operating profit. Then add other income or subtract other expenses, and the result is net profit before taxes. Subtract income taxes, and the bottom line, net profit, is shown.

Chapter 8

What Is Your Overhead Cost per Hour?

Here's the reason for knowing your overhead cost per hour: Assume your company's overhead cost per hour is $50 per hour and your competitor's cost per hour is $25 per hour. For every eight-hour project, your overhead cost is $400, and your competitor's cost is $200.

Your competitor can sell the project for at least $200 less than you can. If your selling prices are similar, then your competitor is earning $200 more on the project than you are. Either way, your costs are much higher than your competitor's costs.

If your overhead is too high because of spending too much on extras and fancy offices, that is one issue that can be resolved. However, if you've "cut your overhead to the bone," then look at other situations.

Let's assume that your overhead costs are similar. Assume your competitor is spreading his overhead cost among eight revenue-producing employees, and you are only spreading it between two revenue-producing employees. Your competitor has a lower overhead cost per employee.

Or, if your competitor's sales volume is two to three times higher than yours, your competitor's overhead per sales dollar is much lower than yours.

Finally, if your competitor's employees are more productive than your employees, his overhead cost per hour will be lower than yours. Generally, the more productive your employees are, the lower your overhead cost per hour.

If you do not have different departments, then to calculate your overhead per hour, take your total overhead cost from last year's fiscal-year-end profit and loss statement. Divide that by the number of revenue-producing labor hours last year (the same revenue-producing hours as in chapter 2).

If you have different departments, then you must departmentalize overhead to calculate each department's overhead cost per hour. Each department must get "its fair share" to arrive at an accurate overhead cost, which then can help you arrive at accurate selling prices for that department's products. I calculate departmentalized overhead based on space costs and labor costs, because they are the two components that create overhead.

Departmentalization can be the greatest source of discussion and disagreement among owners and managers. I've had managers in a room fighting over the number of dollars that they are going to have to pay for each overhead item.

How do you departmentalize overhead so that each department gets its fair share of the amount of overhead that should be allocated to that particular department?

Some companies departmentalize by sales volume. This probably isn't fair, because it's rare that two departments with the same sales volume have equal numbers of employees producing that sales volume.

Take two departments:

	Department A	Department B
Sales	$500,000	$500,000
Revenue producing personnel	2	8
Average revenue per person	$250,000	$40,000

Department B will have more overhead simply because it takes more office people to support Department B than Department A (more billing, phone calls, customers, etc., to produce the $500,000).

If you calculated overhead based on sales in this scenario, Department A and B would get equal overhead allocations. But Department B should receive a higher overhead allocation, because it uses more office resources than Department A.

Now you understand why departmentalizing your overhead expenses should not be done on sales volume. Here's another misconception: you can ignore overhead when pricing your products and service. This occurs when you only use gross margin to calculate your prices.

In the traditional pricing calculations, many companies that sell materials and equipment are taught to determine their prices based on gross margins. I found that this can be a disservice to the companies for many reasons. First, gross margin doesn't tell the whole story. It covers only the direct costs for the products. And, it is a percentage, not actual dollars. If the company margins are high enough, you are probably safe. However, I've known companies who achieve a 55 percent gross margin on a project and still lose money on that project. I've known companies who achieve a 10 percent gross margin for a project, and that project was profitable. Without understanding the "behind the scenes" calculations, i.e., overhead costs, many company owners think that if they achieve a specific gross margin, that's all they have to do to earn a profit. They are ecstatic if they achieve a 50 percent gross margin. Yet that 50 percent margin may not be enough to ensure profitability. You must look at the dollars behind the percentages.

Here's an example. Assume that your company's overhead averages $100,000 per month. One month you generate $250,000 at a 40 percent gross margin. You might think the 40 percent is good. It's neither good or bad. Look at the numbers behind the percentages. To calculate what actually happened during this month, calculate the actual gross profit: $250,000 times 40 percent, or $100,000. Since overhead is $100,000, your company only broke even for the month. Many times in slower revenue-producing months, even with great gross margins, your sales are not high enough to cover your company's monthly overhead.

Understanding your overhead cost per hour and gross profit per hour are critical. Not understanding this is how you can achieve a gross margin of even 50 percent and still lose money on a job. Here's another example.

Assume that your employee performs a service for Mrs. Jones. He charges her $300 for 3 hours of work. Your company gross margin is 50 percent. Your overhead cost per hour is $60. The gross profit for the work your employee performed is $300 times 50 percent, or $150. Your gross profit per hour is $150 divided by 3 hours. This means your gross profit per hour is $50. Your overhead cost per hour is $60 per hour, so you actually lost $10 per hour, or $30, on that project.

Usually you get an eye-opening experience the first time you calculate your overhead costs per hour for your company and each of your departments. At first, you may be estimating some of the overhead costs. Make the best estimates you can. Then you can refine the costs as you increase productivity and get more exact with each overhead item.

When you review your financial statements at the end of the first fiscal year of calculating by overhead cost per hour, you probably will refine the costs per hour for each department. The costs per hour get more accurate as the years go by.

How to Calculate Overhead Cost per Hour

Here is the procedure to calculate the overhead costs per hour for Departments A, B, and C. The answers to the overhead costs per hour will be included in your calculations for each department's retail or project prices. You can use the same exercise if you have more than three departments. Just expand your Excel sheet to include the number of departments your company has.

Overall, determine the overhead costs for each department, and divide that result by the number of productive hours for each department. Even if your company doesn't have departments, use your total company overhead and hours. Divide your total overhead last year by the total number of productive hours (i.e., revenue-generating hours that you calculated in chapter

2). Use only the hours your field employees actually worked for customers.

If you have departments, then do the same calculation as described above for the overhead for each department. You're likely to find one department with a much lower overhead cost per hour than another. After this calculation, you know how little you can charge a customer in slower times of the year and still make a profit on an individual project.

The result can be very sobering. It's common for me to find this number above $60 per hour in many companies I start working with. The idea is to identify it, get it down to a reasonable number, and compete!

How do you get the overhead cost per hour down? By having as many revenue-producing hours as possible. If you pay an employee for eight hours, but he only can bill a customer for four hours, you'll have a higher overhead cost per hour. One of the best ways is to ask your employees. They know how they waste time. Many times you have to ask the office employees about the field employees, and vice versa. They know. Implement their suggestions.

Generally, the first time you do this allocation, your estimates will be just that, estimates. In a few months, everyone will be conscious of the amount of time spent in each department, and the percentages will get more accurate.

Department managers must realize that as their department grows, their department will receive a bigger share of the overhead simply because of its growth. I've worked with many companies who want to grow a smaller department. Initially that department's overhead percentage is small and the actual overhead expenses are little, compared to the other departments. Once this department grows, the overhead percentage gets bigger, and finally that department manager says to me, "I don't want to pay that much overhead." Unfortunately, increasing overhead is a fact of life when a department grows.

Many times the departmentalization calculations are eye opening for managers because for the first time they have to look at the productivity of each office employee. When they realize that their department must pay a portion of that person's salary and benefits, they sometimes speak up, saying, "That person isn't productive, and I shouldn't have to pay for him or her."

Here is how to calculate overhead based on space and people expenses.

First, the space overhead. There are five things that cause space expenses: rent, utilities, building maintenance, building taxes, and building insurance. Determine the total amount of productive space used by each department. Productive space is the space occupied by either people or things related to a revenue-producing department. This does not include your common areas such as a conference room and bathrooms, your bookkeeping space, or your reception space. The space used by financial people or other people who do not produce revenue do not count. The only area that counts is the revenue-producing space of each department.

Using the example in Figure 4, this company has three departments. The building they are located in has 6,000 square feet of revenue-producing space: 2,000 square feet used by Department A, 500 square feet by Department B, and 3,500 square feet by Department C. Department A has been assigned 33.3 percent of the space-related overhead, Department B 8.3 percent, and Department C 58.4 percent. Rent is $72,000 per year. Department

A's portion is $24,000, Department B's is $6,000, and Department C's is $42,000 per year.

Next, people overhead. Every overhead item not included as space overhead is related to people. The more people you have, the more office supplies you have. The more people you have, the more telephone calls that you have.

If you know the exact amount of time that somebody spends in a particular department, then take that percentage rather than the overall estimate shown in this example. If your bookkeeper is splitting her time between three departments, determine how much time she is spending in each department on its tasks and then allocate her salary appropriately.

If things are bought only for one department, then that department gets 100 percent of that expense, such as advertising or printing. Many times advertisements are placed for only one department. As such, that department receives all of that advertising expense. For website expenses, divide the expense by the productive payroll percentages. It's hard to determine if a department should get more or less of that expense.

For people-overhead items that are split, you must determine the total amount of productive payroll. Again using Figure 4, this company's total productive payroll is $750,000. Department A's payroll is $200,000, Department B's payroll is $50,000, and Department C's payroll is $500,000. Department A receives 26.7 percent of the people-related overhead expenses, Department B receives 6.7 percent of the people-related overhead expenses, and Department C receives 66.7 percent of the people-related overhead expenses. That is how each department gets its share of the overhead. If office salaries are $250,000 per year, then Department

A's portion of the overhead is $66,666.67, Department B's is $16,667, and Department C's is $166,667.67.

Once you know the total amount of overhead for each department, then calculate the overhead cost per hour by dividing each department's overhead by its productive labor hours. Department A's total overhead is $303,173.33, with 10,000 total productive hours. Department A's overhead cost per hour is $30.32.

How do you use this to calculate your pricing? Using Figure 4, assume that the company must determine its break-even price for widgets produced in Department C. It takes two hours to produce a widget. The direct cost to produce the widget is $45. Use the profit-and-loss formula described in chapter 7. Net operating profit is zero at break even. Cost of sales is $45.00; overhead is $25.78 per hour, or $51.56 to produce the widget. The break-even sales price is $45 plus $51.56, or $96.56. Your company must sell the widget for more than $96.56 to earn a profit.

Department A provides consulting services. It is proposing a project to a client. The project is estimated to take 80 hours. The salary for the person performing the project is $2,000 per week, or $50 per hour. What is the break-even price to charge the client? The total direct cost is $50 per hour multiplied by 80 hours, or $4,000. The overhead cost is 80 hours multiplied by $30.32 per hour, or $2,425.60. The break-even proposal price is $4,000 plus $2,425.60, or $6,425.60.

What about profit? Determine the net profit per hour the department should earn (see chapter 2), and add that amount to the break-even price. If the desired net profit per hour in Department C is $15 per hour, then the net profit needed for that widget is $15 multiplied by 2 hours, or $30.00. The selling price is $96.56 plus $30.00, or $126.56.

If the desired net profit per hour for Department A is $75 per hour, then the net profit needed for that project is $75 multiplied by 80 hours, or $6,000. The proposal investment to the client is $6,000 plus $6,425.60, or $12,425.60.

Only you can determine the net profit per hour you are comfortable with. It might depend on competitive pricing and the perceived value you provide to your customers.

GETTING STARTED ON OVERHEAD COST PER HOUR CALCULATIONS

Take your year-end W-2s, which list the total payroll for each employee. Separate the employees into the different departments. Total the payroll for each department. Remember that you are only interested in productive payroll. If you have salespeople, include their salaries in the department they sell for. Also, if an employee works in two departments, estimate the amount of time that he spends in each of the departments and allocate his payroll accordingly. For example, if one of your employees earned $50,000 last year, and he spent 20 percent of his time in Department A and 80 percent of his time Department B, then 80 percent of $50,000, or $40,000, would be allocated to Department B, and 20 percent of $50,000, or $10,000, would be allocated to Department A.

Once you have all the departments' payroll, then add all the departments together to determine the total productive payroll. Each department gets a percentage based on its payroll divided by the total payroll.

Overhead Cost Per Hour Example

	Dept A	Dept B	Dept C	TOTALS
Occupied Space (sq.ft.)	2,000	500	3,500	6,000.00
Space Percentages	33.3%	8.3%	58.3%	
Productive Labor ($)	200,000	50,000	500,000	750,000.00
Labor Percentages	26.7%	6.7%	66.7%	
Productive Labor (hours)	10,000	3,333	28,000	41,333.00
Overhead Expenses				
Advertising & marketing	26,666.67	6,666.67	66,666.67	100,000.00
Bad debts	533.33	133.33	1,333.33	2,000.00
Building Maintenance	6,666.67	1,666.67	11,666.67	20,000.00
Computer support	1,333.33	333.33	3,333.33	5,000.00
Contributions/donations	533.33	133.33	1,333.33	2,000.00
Depreciation Expense	2,666.67	666.67	6,666.67	10,000.00
Fines & Penalties	0.00	0.00	0.00	0.00
Insurance - TOTAL	40,000.00	10,000.00	100,000.00	150,000.00
Interest Expense	533.33	133.33	1,333.33	2,000.00
Licenses & Permits	266.67	66.67	666.67	1,000.00
Meetings	800.00	200.00	2,000.00	3,000.00
Miscellaneous	266.67	66.67	666.67	1,000.00
Morale & Incentives	1,200.00	300.00	3,000.00	4,500.00
Office Expense	1,733.33	433.33	4,333.33	6,500.00
Outside services	4,000.00	1,000.00	10,000.00	15,000.00
Postage & Delivery	533.33	133.33	1,333.33	2,000.00
Printing	1,333.33	333.33	3,333.33	5,000.00
Prof Fees	6,666.67	1,666.67	16,666.67	25,000.00
Profit Sharing Plan	1,333.33	333.33	3,333.33	5,000.00
Rent - Building	24,000.00	6,000.00	42,000.00	72,000.00
Rent - other equipment	2,133.33	533.33	5,333.33	8,000.00
Repairs & maint - building	666.67	166.67	1,166.67	2,000.00
Repairs & maint - other	133.33	33.33	333.33	500.00
Salaries - Office	66,666.67	16,666.67	166,666.67	250,000.00
Salaries - officers	40,000.00	10,000.00	100,000.00	150,000.00
Salaries - payroll service	533.33	133.33	1,333.33	2,000.00
Security Expense	320.00	80.00	800.00	1,200.00
Shipping and freight	800.00	200.00	2,000.00	3,000.00
Supplies & Small Tools	3,733.33	933.33	9,333.33	14,000.00
Taxes - Property	2,000.00	500.00	3,500.00	6,000.00
Taxes - payroll	13,866.67	3,466.67	34,666.67	52,000.00
Taxes - other	533.33	133.33	1,333.33	2,000.00
Telephone - office	6,400.00	1,600.00	16,000.00	24,000.00
Telephone - pagers/radios	1,600.00	400.00	4,000.00	6,000.00
Training & education	3,200.00	800.00	8,000.00	12,000.00
Travel	1,066.67	266.67	2,666.67	4,000.00
Entertainment	266.67	66.67	666.67	1,000.00
Unapplied time	800.00	200.00	2,000.00	3,000.00
Uniforms	1,386.67	346.67	3,466.67	5,200.00
Utilities	8,000.00	2,000.00	14,000.00	24,000.00
Vehicles - gas & oil	18,666.67	4,666.67	46,666.67	70,000.00
Vehicles - maintenance	5,333.33	1,333.33	13,333.33	20,000.00
Vehicles - leases	2,666.67	666.67	6,666.67	10,000.00
TOTAL OVERHEAD EXP	301,840.00	75,460.00	723,600.00	1,100,900.00
OVERHEAD COST/HR	30.18	22.64	25.84	

Figure 4. Overhead Cost per Hour Format

Estimate the space requirements for each department. Each department receives its space-overhead percentage based on the total productive space.

Then get your latest fiscal-year-end's financial statements, showing the total overhead for the year. Using the spreadsheet titled Overhead Cost per Hour (you can download the spreadsheets at www.thecouragetobeprofitable.com/downloads), enter the totals of each overhead expense in the gray areas. Then determine which expenses are space-related overhead expenses and which are people-related overhead expenses. In Figure 4, the space-related overhead expenses are building rent, building repairs and maintenance, building insurance, property taxes, and utilities. The rest are people-related overhead expenses.

Final Thoughts on Overhead Cost

If your overhead cost per hour is too high, you have two choices: decrease overhead (usually harder to do), or increase sales at the same level of overhead.

Once you reach a certain level of overhead, it is very difficult to decrease it. You get comfortable with it, and losing a person could be very difficult to overcome.

Remember, the lower your overhead cost per hour, the better you are able to compete. Be as efficient as you possibly can.

Relying only on gross margins to determine whether a project went well or not is dangerous. You have to know and understand what your overhead cost per hour is. The only thing that really counts is the net profit per hour that you are generating. That's what you can convert to cash and take to the bank.

IMPLEMENT
YOUR BUSINESS
FINANCIAL REVIEW

Chapter 9

What Do I Really Need to Do?

There are three major activities that you must do:

1. Weekly cash-flow report
2. Monthly financial ratio analysis
3. Monthly trend analyses

Your bookkeeper should produce a cash-flow report for you each week. If you don't have a bookkeeper, you need to invest the fifteen minutes each week to create the report.

The financial ratio analysis and trend analyses are analyzed monthly after you receive your financial statements. It usually takes thirty minutes or less to complete this critical analysis. Financial statements should be completed by the fifteenth of the following month. Timeliness is critical. If you receive January's statement in April, it's too late to take action on what happened months ago.

In addition, looking at one month's financial statements (balance sheet and profit and loss statement) does not tell the total story. You must look at your business trends. They are more important because they show where the business is headed. When you review the graphs explained in this chapter, you can choose to continue on the current path the graphs are showing you, or make the necessary changes to alter the direction of your business.

1. WEEKLY CASH-FLOW REPORT

A weekly cash-flow report helps you track the cash coming in and going out of your business. Your bookkeeper puts this statement on your desk every Friday afternoon, along with a copy of the company's accounts receivable and accounts payable list. They should take no longer than fifteen minutes to prepare, assuming that accounts receivable and accounts payable are up to date. The weekly cash-flow report format is shown in Figure 5.

Beginning cash is the cash you have at the start of the week; *petty cash* is the cash in your operating checking accounts, payroll checking account, and money market funds. It is not stock investments or long-term investments. It's cash. It's what you use to cover checks you've written.

Next determine your cash receipts for the week. You receive cash when your clients pay you for work performed—i.e., when you collect on sales. Collections on sales come in many forms. You may receive cash, credit card payments, and checks. Each is tracked as a separate line item. Cash is generated by collections on sales, not by sending the invoice to the customer.

Inputs are cash that the company receives this week. *Other inputs* might include investment income or borrowing from the bank line of credit. There might be an investment in the business (i.e., an owner made a loan to the company or sold additional stock). There might be a sale of an asset where you received cash for that asset.

Disbursements are cash going out of the company this week. Disbursements are the checks written for accounts payable, payroll, loan payments, purchases of inventory and other assets, and payment of overhead expenses.

Ending cash is simply beginning cash, plus inputs, minus disbursements. Ending cash must be positive (i.e., there must be water left in the tank). Without enough cash, you need to decide who isn't getting paid. Sometimes those are the tough decisions. Have the courage to make them.

The weekly cash-flow statement starts with beginning cash and adds collections for the week to get the total cash available for the week. Then disbursements are subtracted to get the ending cash for the week. Then take it one step further: plan for the following week.

Estimate accounts receivables that are going to be collected, payables and loan payments that must be paid, and what payroll will be. Then take ending cash for this week, subtract payroll for next week and disbursements for next week, and add expected collections for next week. The end result should be a positive number. If it's not, time must be spent on collections or deciding which vendor isn't going to get paid.

The weekly cash-flow report forces your company to be current (up to date with entries) for receivables and payables entries each

WEEKLY CASH REPORT

Week of _____   Prepared by _____

Cash on hand at the beginning of the week:

Petty Cash $ _____
Checking account #1 $ _____
Checking account #2: $ _____
Payroll account $ _____
Money Market $ _____
Other savings $ _____

                    Total beginning cash $ _____

Cash Collected $ _____
Credit card payments Collected $ _____
Accounts Receivable Collected $ _____
Other Infusions (loans etc.) $ _____

TOTAL AVAILABLE CASH FOR THE WEEK $ _____

Disbursements:

Payroll $ _____
Accounts Payable $ _____
Loan payments $ _____
Other $ _____

                    Total Disbursements $ _____

ENDING CASH FOR WEEK $ _____

Estimated requirements for next week:

Accounts receivable to be collected : $ _____
Payroll $ _____
Accounts payable to be paid $ _____
Loan payments due $ _____

TOTAL ESTIMATED CASH SURPLUS (NEEDS) NEXT WEEK $ _____

Figure 5. Weekly Cash-Flow Report

week. This makes it easier to produce timely monthly financial statements each month.

As previously stated, your bookkeeper should put this statement on your desk each Friday afternoon. If that number is negative (i.e., you need more cash next week), it's a lot easier to have a week to collect that cash than that bookkeeper knocking on your door Thursday saying, "We don't have enough to make payroll," and payroll is due on Friday.

2. MONTHLY FINANCIAL RATIO ANALYSIS

There are ten ratios that I use for analyzing companies' financial statements. These ratios help you operate your business on a day-to-day basis. They are not necessarily what a banker is used to seeing, or expects. My answer to a banker is this: "If these ratios are within acceptable limits for our industry, any ratio that you, the banker, wants is going to be within acceptable limits for our industry." So if a banker wants you to calculate a return on assets or return on investments, you can very easily calculate those ratio calculations in addition to these ten ratios.

These ten ratios are operational ratios. They tell you instantly what is going on with your business. You'll know whether your employees are productive. You'll know if you have or may soon have a cash-flow problem. You'll know if you're using your inventory properly. You'll be able to tell whether you have too much debt. The ratios are used to determine the health of your company. It is important to compute these financial ratios on a monthly basis, because the trends are as important as the specific monthly figures. You can help your company avert a potential crisis by examining these ratios each month.

Current Ratio

This ratio is a measure of liquidity—i.e., how easily can your company pay its bills? Calculate this ratio by using figures from the balance sheet. The ratio is:

$$\frac{\textbf{Current Assets}}{\textbf{Current Liabilities}}$$

The current ratio answers the question, "Is your business liquid enough so that you can pay your bills on a timely basis?" Current assets are things that are cash or turned into cash within a year. Current liabilities are things that you have to pay within a year. Do not include owner receivables or payables that will not be repaid within a year. Check the Risk Management Association's (formerly Robert Morris Associates) *Annual Statement Studies* for the average ratios in your industry.

Assume that you calculate the current ratio, and it is 1.95. Is that good or bad? It actually depends. If you compare it to the standard industry ratio of 1.50, the ratio looks good. However, you should compare the ratio to your previous month's ratio. If the month before you had a current ratio of 2.05, and it went down to 1.95 this month, that's not good because the ratio is trending the wrong way. Or if the previous month was 1.65 and it went to 1.95 this month, your company is doing better. You are going in the right direction.

With these ratios, you have to look at the trend. A single figure won't tell you too much. Are the ratios going the right way, or are the ratios going the wrong way?

A decreasing current ratio is the first indication of lessening profitability. If the current ratio is decreasing, ninety times out of a hundred that means your profitability is decreasing. You are likely to have a higher percentage of expenses as compared to revenues, which means higher current liabilities as compared to current assets.

The other major reason you might have a decreasing current ratio is that you bought a long-term asset. For example, if you paid cash for a vehicle, then you've decreased cash, which is a current asset item, and you created a long-term asset—i.e., a vehicle. So your cash decreased, and your long-term assets increased. When your cash decreases and your current liabilities stay the same, your current ratio decreases. The same thing would happen if you purchased equipment, office furniture, or a building. You are converting current assets into long-term assets, which reduces your current ratio.

On a positive note, if your current ratio is increasing, then you are becoming more profitable. If your current ratio is staying about the same, your profitability is probably staying about the same. But a sale of assets might also increase your current ratio. If you sold a truck, you are transferring a long-term asset (i.e., a truck) to a current asset (i.e., cash). Your current ratio would increase in this situation. However, the main reason that current ratio increases most of the time is that profitability is increasing.

Acid Test, or Quick Ratio

The next measure of liquidity is called the acid test, or the quick ratio. If your company has no inventory, your acid test equals your current ratio. Do not calculate this ratio if your company has no inventory. Bankers have said, "Many companies have too much money tied up in inventory." Bankers want to see what happens to the current ratio when inventory is taken out of the equation—i.e., can the company still pay its bills?

Calculate this ratio by using figures from the balance sheet. It is calculated:

$$\frac{\text{Current Assets} - \text{Inventory}}{\text{Current Liabilities}}$$

Again, check the Risk Management Association's *Annual Statement Studies* for the average ratios for your industry. Like the current ratio, if you have a decreasing acid test, you are not as profitable or you bought some assets. If you have an increasing acid test, you are more profitable or you sold some assets. Generally the acid test follows the same trend as the current ratio.

If your current ratio is changing and your acid test is staying the same from month to month, or vice versa, this means that your inventory is changing. If your current ratio is the same and the acid test is decreasing, then you are trading cash for inventory. Be very careful. Inventory is a bet and can drain your cash.

When calculating the acid test, only include assets that are cash or turned into cash within one year in the current asset total. Include only items that must be paid within a year in the current liabilities total (see current ratio for a detailed explanation).

Accounts Receivable to Accounts Payable (AR/AP)

This ratio is a measure of liquidity. Calculate this ratio by looking at figures from the balance sheet. It is calculated:

$$\frac{\text{Trade Receivables}}{\text{Trade Payables}}$$

receivables by your trade payables. Do ~~receivables, employee payables, owner's~~ ~~...yables.~~ Trade receivables only include the ... people or companies owe your company. Trade payables include the amount owed to vendors and other people to whom your company owes money.

If more than 50 percent of your sales are collected on a COD basis, add accounts receivables plus cash, and divide that sum by accounts payable. Here is the reason: if you just divide receivables by payables and most of your business is COD, your company has almost no receivables and "normal" payables. The division would make the ratio near zero. It wouldn't be telling the right story, since your company has received cash for the work that it has done well in advance of the time that it has to pay the payables for the work that was done. For COD companies, when cash is included in the ratio, the ratio becomes "normal" again and realistic. COD is a great way to manage cash. However, it is not practical for some companies.

What does the accounts receivable to accounts payable ratio mean? If you have an increasing ratio, you have more billed projects, more profits, more COD projects, or less collections. (For those companies on a COD basis, there are no collections, so this cannot be a reason for an increasing ratio.) Check out why the ratio is increasing. Less collections is not good. The receivable days ratio, discussed later in this chapter, helps you determine if you have less collections.

If you have a decreasing accounts receivable to accounts payable, you have less billing, less COD, less profits, or more collections. Find out which event is occurring, and have the courage to take action when you find less billing less profits.

Debt to Equity

This ratio looks at the amount of debt that the company is burdened with. Calculate this ratio by looking at the balance sheet. It is calculated:

$$\frac{\text{Total Liabilities}}{\text{Total Equity}}$$

Total debt is total liabilities: both current liabilities and long-term liabilities. Divide total liabilities by the equity, or the total net worth of the business. The result should be greater than zero but as low as possible.

The debt-to-equity ratio doesn't have "an average value." I've seen this ratio as high as 11—and the company was still profitable. Most of the time when the debt-to-equity ratio increases dramatically, several large, long-term projects are in their initial stages. The company is purchasing significant quantities of equipment and materials. When this happens, you'll also see a high jump in accounts receivable as the company bills for these materials. If your current ratio and your acid test are moving in the right direction, your long-term debt to equity is in the proper range (which I'll discuss next), and your percentage compensation is within averages (which I'll discuss later), the value of your debt-to-equity ratio is not that important, because the company can service the debt (i.e., it can pay its bills).

So regard this ratio as a warning ratio. It should not "jump up" or increase rapidly. It should be consistent or decreasing. If it is increasing, that is a warning sign that the company isn't paying its bills or has incurred too much debt. A decreasing debt-to-equity ratio means that profitability is increasing and the company is paying off debt. If the debt-to-equity ratio is increasing, the company has decreased profitability and is incurring more debt. Watch this ratio not for the numbers specifically, but whether it is increasing or decreasing. That's really the key to ensuring your company isn't taking on too much debt.

A final note about the debt-to-equity ratio. It should definitely not be negative! If the ratio is negative, it means that the net worth of the company is negative—i.e., it has more liabilities than assets. If the company is seeking a bank loan, very few bankers will extend loans when a company has a negative net worth, unless there are extenuating circumstances, and there are assets that the company can pledge. A negative net worth means that the company is probably in trouble, because it has been losing money for a long period of time.

Long-Term Debt to Equity

This financial ratio looks at how much long-term debt the company owes. Calculate this ratio by looking at the balance sheet. It is calculated:

$$\frac{\textbf{Long-Term Liabilities}}{\textbf{Total Equity}}$$

Again, make sure that items that should be in long-term liabilities are there. If there are bank loans, and the current portion of these loans is included, then this ratio will be overstated.

In most cases, this ratio should be greater than zero and less than one. It should definitely not be negative! (See the explanation for debt to equity.)

The long-term debt to equity ratio looks at long-term liabilities divided by equity. It tells whether the company is burdened with huge amounts of long-term debts that will be paid over many years. You want this amount of debt to be as low as possible.

If you have a decreasing long-term debt to equity (which is good), your company will have either increasing profitability or be paying off some of its long-term debts. If this ratio is increasing, then this is a warning sign. The company has decreasing profitability and is incurring more debt.

Productivity Ratio (Percentage Compensation)

This ratio is my favorite ratio. This ratio answers the question: for each dollar in revenue that the company earns, how much is the company spending on payroll and payroll taxes? It tells you how productive your employees are. Calculate this ratio by looking at the profit and loss statement. It is calculated:

$$\frac{\text{Total payroll plus payroll taxes}}{\text{Sales}}$$

Payroll includes all payroll: field labor, office labor, owner's salaries, etc. In some cases, if your company uses subcontracted labor, this should be included as well. Payroll taxes include

FICA, Medicare, and state and federal unemployment taxes. It does not include health insurance, 401(k) or other retirement plans, or bonuses.

The companies that don't manage labor well tend to be less profitable or operate at a loss most of the time.

Bankers rarely track this ratio because they don't understand how critical productive labor is to most companies. If they did, they would require this ratio in their analyses.

Percentage compensation looks at only payroll and payroll costs. This includes direct wages for the entire company, plus payroll taxes. Many companies make the mistake of including year-end bonuses in this calculation. The percentage compensation looks at operating requirements. Bonuses are not required in your day-to-day operations. They are given voluntarily at the end of a period in addition to regular wages for a specific reason.

This is the only ratio that can be calculated by department to monitor the labor productivity of each department. If you calculate this ratio by department, it assumes that you have departmentalized the overhead and each department is getting its fair share (see chapter 8). In addition, if you calculate this ratio at the end of the year, calculate it on the payroll for normal operations. Do not include bonuses; they are not part of operating expenses.

In a very busy time of the year, there may be overtime paid to employees. In many cases, you can't charge the customer an overtime rate. As a result, the percentage compensation ratio increases. Yes, you can be busy and earn less profits.

The reason I like the percentage compensation ratio is that I can see whether a company's employees are productive just by this one ratio. If the percentage compensation is decreasing, it's going the right way. The company has less unapplied time or less overtime (or been able to bill most of the overtime). Company sales are increasing as compared to labor expense. It might mean that revenues per project are increasing, the field employees are spending more time on the project rather than driving to the project, or the company is able to bill out more hours for every hour that employees are charging the company (i.e., an employee is charging the company eight hours, and it can bill the customer eight hours).

Receivable Turns

The next two ratios are receivable turns and receivable days. I look at these two ratios together, because receivable turns don't mean too much to me in an intuitive sense. I can "see" receivable days. I know that the receivable days are the number of days between the time your company sends out an invoice and receives payment for that invoice.

These ratios measure how efficiently the company collects its receivables. The turns are calculated on annual sales. Calculate this ratio by using both the income statement and the balance sheet. It is calculated:

$$\frac{\textbf{Annualized Sales}}{\textbf{Trade Accounts Receivable}}$$

To annualize sales, multiply the year-to-date sales by 12 and divide it by the month of the fiscal year that you are in. So for example, if year-to-date sales are $100,000 and the company is in month 5 of its fiscal year, multiply $100,000 by 12 and divide that by 5. Then divide that number by trade accounts receivable. Use only the trade accounts receivable—the amounts that customers owe the company. Do not include employee receivables or owner receivables.

Like the accounts receivable to accounts payable ratio, if more than 50 percent of the revenues are COD revenues, then use accounts receivable plus cash as the divisor.

Now calculate receivable days.

Receivable Days

This figure also measures how efficiently the company collects its receivables. The days are calculated from the receivable turns figure. It is calculated:

$$\frac{365}{\textbf{Receivable Turns}}$$

If receivable days are increasing, that means more billing, less COD sales, and less collections.

On the other hand, if the ratio is decreasing, there is less billing, more COD, or more collections activities. Try to maintain receivable days under forty-five days, and if the company has mainly COD revenues, under thirty days.

Pay attention to receivable days. If they continue to increase, you have a collection problem. Have the courage to call your customers with overdue accounts and find out when you will be getting payment for the work you completed. Or, if you hire someone to handle collections, make sure you review your accounts receivable list every week and get progress reports on collection activities.

Inventory Turns

The last two ratios are inventory turns and inventory days. Remember, these values are zero if your company has no inventory. Don't calculate these two ratios if you company does not have inventory. Like receivable turns, I rely on the "turns" to get the "days." Inventory days is the number of days between the time a part is purchased to the time it is used on a project. Inventory turns are calculated on annualized costs. Calculate this ratio by using both the income statement and the balance sheet. It is calculated:

$$\frac{\text{Annualized Material Expense}}{\text{Inventory}}$$

For many construction companies, I calculate the ratio on cost of goods sold rather than just material expense. The reason is that for many construction companies, labor is an integral factor in inventory usage. It is rare to find a company that can install or service a part or piece of equipment without labor expense.

To annualize material expense or cost of goods sold, multiply the year-to-date cost of goods sold by 12 and divide by the month of the fiscal year you are in. So if you're in month 7 of your fiscal year, take the year-to-date cost of goods sold, multiply by 12, divide by 7, and that's the number to divide the inventory into.

Can seasonality affect this ratio? Perhaps. My feeling is that since you are annualizing the sales or cost of sales, then the annualization is not seasonal. The important thing is to look at the trends and see what is happening with the ratios. The ratios might be higher after a spring or fall season. However, you'll notice this year after year and come to expect it.

Now calculate inventory days.

Inventory Days

This financial ratio measures the average time a part is in your warehouse before it's used. Calculate this ratio from the inventory-turn number. It is calculated:

$$\frac{365}{\textbf{Inventory Turns}}$$

If inventory days are increasing, this is a warning sign. There is more purchasing, less usage, or perhaps stocking orders issues.

Inventory is a bet. Don't stock more than you think you can reasonably sell. Be very wise and thoughtful in how you purchase inventory. You are betting your hard-earned dollars that you will be able to sell it. I have seen a lot of bad bets over the years with obsolete inventory.

If you have decreasing inventory days, you have less purchasing and more usage. That's exactly the trend you want to see until inventory days stabilize at a certain number. You want the lowest reasonable inventory levels. Obviously you don't want someone running to a supplier every five minutes. You need a reasonable level of inventory that you can turn or that you can use in a reasonable amount of time.

Receivable Days to Inventory Days

Finally, look at receivable days to inventory days. Receivable days should always be greater than inventory days. For companies with no inventory, inventory days are zero, so your receivable days will always be greater than your inventory days. If you have thirty days

Month	TotSales	TotGP	OH	Net Op. Prft
Jan 08	$459,318	$33,030	$74,818	$41,788
Feb 08	$308,454	$60,158	$93,258	-$33,100
Mar 08	$266,573	$142,809	$36,219	$106,589
Apr 08	$265,413	$45,969	$77,273	-$31,303
May 08	$255,990	$152,993	$87,208	$65,784
Jun 08	$221,592	$78,777	$102,706	-$23,928
Jul 08	$617,619	$266,289	$101,617	$164,672
Aug 08	$395,553	$41,482	$85,460	-$43,977
Sep 08	$324,901	$76,620	$91,184	-$14,563
Oct 08	$413,271	-$40,788	$85,856	-$126,644
Nov 08	$314,858	$51,417	$114,953	-$63,536
Dec 08	$291,590	$44,225	$76,702	-$32,476
Jan 09	$272,722	$47,643	$73,203	-$25,560
Feb 09	$160,545	$5,533	$72,004	-$66,470
Mar 09	$280,261	$76,779	$65,998	$10,781
Apr 09	$357,174	$104,087	$71,545	$32,541
May 09	$418,746	$84,193	$67,939	$16,253
Jun 09	$392,997	$95,825	$87,713	$8,111
Jul 09	$490,000	$80,487	$93,843	-$13,355
Aug 09	$320,431	$300,501	$50,402	$250,098
Sep 09	$262,834	$32,714	$70,590	-$37,876
Oct 09	$476,498	$108,218	$66,549	$41,668
Nov 09	$349,848	$45,877	$189,776	-$143,898
Dec 09	$380,397	$62,453	$106,358	-$41,113
Jan 10	$251,800	$52,249	$62,312	-$7,416
Feb 10	$207,031	$22,146	$83,002	-$59,013
Mar 10	$351,281	$109,836	$73,567	$37,938
Apr 10	$313,119	$110,181	$76,392	$36,395
May 10	$334,861	$90,860	$87,528	$5,266
Jun 10	$432,681	$125,543	$101,758	$25,720
Jul 10	$549,951	$188,268	$80,524	$110,877
Aug 10	$332,392	$66,207	$45,821	$22,148
Sep 10	$309,365	$80,411	$80,228	$183
Oct 10	$423,605	$139,437	$90,731	$49,733
Nov 10	$466,964	$106,896	$163,188	-$54,384
Dec 10	$506,792	$98,967	$95,870	$3,097

Figure 6a. Monthly Financial Data Chart

Trailing	TotSales	TotGP	OH	Net Op. Prft
Dec 08	$344,594	$79,415	$85,605	$776
Jan 09	$329,045	$80,633	$85,470	-$4,837
Feb 09	$316,719	$76,081	$83,699	-$7,618
Mar 09	$317,860	$70,578	$86,180	-$15,602
Apr 09	$325,506	$75,421	$85,703	-$10,281
May 09	$339,069	$69,688	$84,097	-$14,409
Jun 09	$353,353	$71,109	$82,848	-$11,739
Jul 09	$342,718	$55,625	$82,200	-$26,575
Aug 09	$336,458	$77,210	$79,279	-$2,068
Sep 09	$331,286	$73,551	$77,562	-$4,011
Oct 09	$336,555	$85,969	$75,953	$10,015
Nov 09	$339,471	$85,507	$82,189	$3,318
Dec 09	$346,871	$87,026	$84,660	$2,598
Jan 10	$345,128	$87,410	$83,752	$4,110
Feb 10	$349,001	$88,794	$84,669	$4,732
Mar 10	$354,920	$91,549	$85,300	$6,995
Apr 10	$351,248	$92,057	$85,704	$7,316
May 10	$344,258	$92,612	$87,336	$6,400
Jun 10	$347,565	$95,089	$88,506	$7,868
Jul 10	$352,561	$104,070	$87,397	$18,221
Aug 10	$353,558	$84,546	$87,015	-$775
Sep 10	$357,435	$88,521	$87,818	$2,396
Oct 10	$353,028	$91,122	$89,833	$3,068
Nov 10	$362,787	$96,207	$87,618	$10,528
Dec 10	$373,320	$99,250	$86,743	$14,212

Figure 6b. Monthly Financial Data Chart

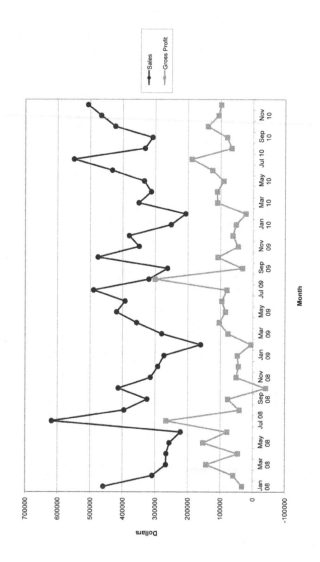

Figure 7a. Monthly Financial Data Graph

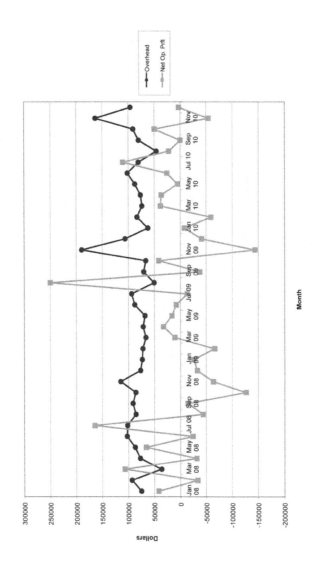

Figure 7b. Monthly Financial Data Graph

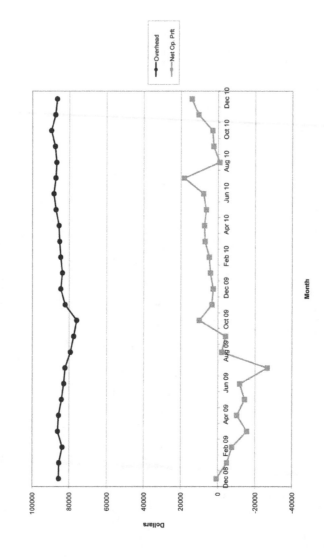

Figure 8a. Trailing Financial Data Graph

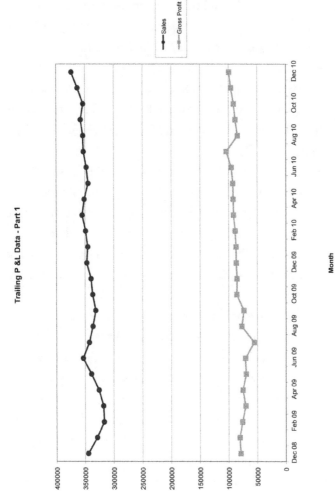

Figure 8b. Trailing Financial Data Graph

You can't tell much by looking at the numbers. However, when you graph the numbers, you can see the trends for this company. Graphing the monthly data, as shown in Figure 7, still doesn't show much other than ups and downs. You can't see the business trends.

However, when you graph the trailing data, the company story emerges, as shown in Figure 8. The templates to create your financial graphs are at www.thecouragetobeprofitable.com/downloads.

The monthly financial data looks like a series of sine waves, or radio waves. You really can't tell what is happening with the company from this graph. When analyzing the graph, total sales and gross profit trends should be parallel. The lines should mirror each other. This means that the company's gross margin is consistent. If it isn't consistent, you have financial fruit salad (see chapter 10).

The trailing data shows an interesting story. For several years, the company's sales and profits declined. This is shown by the decreasing revenue and profit lines. Then they stabilized at a lower range. In the past year, the company has started growing again.

The overhead line should be flat. If it is increasing each month, the company is adding overhead expense. If the sales line is decreasing and the overhead is increasing, you need the courage to cut overhead and turn the sales decline around.

Since the profit-and-loss trailing numbers look at an entire year's data one month at a time, the small changes in trends are significant. Spotting the trends and taking action on them is like turning around an oil tanker—it takes time. This is why it is so critical to take action when you see small changes in the trends.

Financial Ratio Trends

Track the financial ratios on a trailing basis. To graph the current ratio trailing data point for January 2012, add the current ratio each month from February 2011 through January 2012, and divide by 12.

The financial ratio trend graphs are divided into four segments:

- Liquidity
- Debt
- Productivity
- Usage (Receivable Days and Inventory Days)

Figure 9 shows the monthly trailing and liquidity ratio data.

Figure 10 shows the monthly and trailing debt ratios data.

Figure 11 shows the monthly and trailing productivity ratios data.

Figure 12 shows monthly and trailing usage ratio data graphs for the financial ratios.

Figures 13–20 show the monthly and trailing ratio graphs for the financial ratios.

Liquidity Ratio Trends

There are three measures of business liquidity (i.e., can you pay your bills?). These are the current ratio, acid test or quick ratio, and accounts receivable to accounts payable. All of these ratios are found on the balance sheet, as previously stated in this chapter.

An increasing current ratio generally means increasing profitability. A decreasing current ratio generally means decreasing profitability. This is also true with the trends.

Figure 9: Liquidity Ratios

Month	Current	Acid	AR/AP	Trailing	Current	Acid	AR/AP
Jan 09	1.39	1.24	1.57				
Feb 09	1.31	1.18	1.55				
Mar 09	1.72	1.51	1.70				
Apr 09	1.45	1.31	2.27				
May 09	1.68	1.48	1.70				
Jun 09	1.61	1.40	2.02				
Jul 09	1.43	1.26	2.16				
Aug 09	1.26	1.12	1.63				
Sep 09	1.35	1.18	2.13				
Oct 09	1.22	1.08	2.22				
Nov 09	1.16	1.04	1.69				
Dec 09	1.41	1.27	1.55	Dec 09	1.42	1.26	1.85
Jan 10	1.28	1.14	1.41	Jan 10	1.41	1.25	1.84
Feb 10	1.24	1.11	1.65	Feb 10	1.40	1.24	1.84
Mar 10	1.60	1.40	1.93	Mar 10	1.39	1.23	1.86
Apr 10	1.34	1.20	1.56	Apr 10	1.38	1.22	1.80
May 10	1.29	1.19	1.28	May 10	1.35	1.20	1.77
Jun 10	1.24	1.16	1.47	Jun 10	1.32	1.18	1.72
Jul 10	1.18	1.11	1.52	Jul 10	1.30	1.17	1.67
Aug 10	1.19	1.12	1.54	Aug 10	1.29	1.17	1.66
Sep 10	1.16	1.09	1.36	Sep 10	1.28	1.16	1.60
Oct 10	1.17	1.09	1.48	Oct 10	1.27	1.16	1.54
Nov 10	1.14	1.08	1.72	Nov 10	1.27	1.16	1.54

Figure 9. Liquidity Ratios

Figure 10: Debt Ratios

Month	D/E	LTD/E	Trailing	D/E	LTD/E
Jan 09	2.92	0.44			
Feb 09	3.49	0.46			
Mar 09	1.59	0.15			
Apr 09	2.54	0.34			
May 09	1.59	0.24			
Jun 09	1.77	0.28			
Jul 09	2.51	0.28			
Aug 09	3.75	0.35			
Sep 09	2.90	0.32			
Oct 09	4.24	0.38			
Nov 09	6.69	0.67			
Dec 09	2.97	0.41	Dec 09	3.08	0.36
Jan 10	4.38	0.57	Jan 10	3.20	0.37
Feb 10	4.81	0.53	Feb 10	3.31	0.38
Mar 10	1.95	0.28	Mar 10	3.34	0.39
Apr 10	3.14	0.31	Apr 10	3.39	0.39
May 10	3.58	0.25	May 10	3.56	0.39
Jun 10	4.19	0.20	Jun 10	3.76	0.38
Jul 10	5.31	0.23	Jul 10	3.99	0.38
Aug 10	5.00	0.18	Aug 10	4.10	0.36
Sep 10	5.81	0.21	Sep 10	4.34	0.35
Oct 10	5.49	0.21	Oct 10	4.44	0.34
Nov 10	6.52	0.20	Nov 10	4.43	0.30

Figure 10. Debt Ratios

Figure 11: Productivity Ratio

Month	% Comp	Trailing	% Comp
Jan 09	67.0%		
Feb 09	49.0%		
Mar 09	26.0%		
Apr 09	34.0%		
May 09	26.0%		
Jun 09	60.0%		
Jul 09	45.0%		
Aug 09	67.0%		
Sep 09	36.0%		
Oct 09	58.0%		
Nov 09	58.0%		
Dec 09	21.0%	Dec 09	45.6%
Jan 10	61.0%	Jan 10	45.1%
Feb 10	34.0%	Feb 10	43.8%
Mar 10	18.0%	Mar 10	43.2%
Apr 10	26.0%	Apr 10	42.5%
May 10	27.0%	May 10	42.6%
Jun 10	28.0%	Jun 10	39.9%
Jul 10	50.0%	Jul 10	40.3%
Aug 10	31.0%	Aug 10	37.3%
Sep 10	40.0%	Sep 10	37.7%
Oct 10	38.0%	Oct 10	36.0%
Nov 10	35.0%	Nov 10	34.1%

Figure 11. Productivity Ratios

Figure 12: Usage Ratios

Month	AR Days	Inv Days	Trailing	AR Days	Inv Days
Jan 09	80.58	28.22			
Feb 09	61.37	27.89			
Mar 09	33.62	13.49			
Apr 09	52.51	14.20			
May 09	33.62	32.39			
Jun 09	29.42	14.32			
Jul 09	37.18	15.26			
Aug 09	34.26	14.47			
Sep 09	37.73	16.10			
Oct 09	44.81	16.10			
Nov 09	44.18	17.54			
Dec 09	61.56	14.75	Dec 09	45.90	18.73
Jan 10	102.71	27.50	Jan 10	47.75	18.67
Feb 10	66.63	20.41	Feb 10	48.19	18.04
Mar 10	46.63	13.38	Mar 10	49.27	18.04
Apr 10	46.37	14.24	Apr 10	48.76	18.04
May 10	53.15	13.41	May 10	50.39	16.46
Jun 10	69.85	13.72	Jun 10	53.76	16.41
Jul 10	72.72	15.25	Jul 10	56.72	16.41
Aug 10	61.39	15.27	Aug 10	58.98	16.47
Sep 10	53.94	14.82	Sep 10	60.33	16.37
Oct 10	35.67	13.69	Oct 10	59.57	16.17
Nov 10	56.89	15.30	Nov 10	60.63	15.98

Figure 12. Usage Ratios

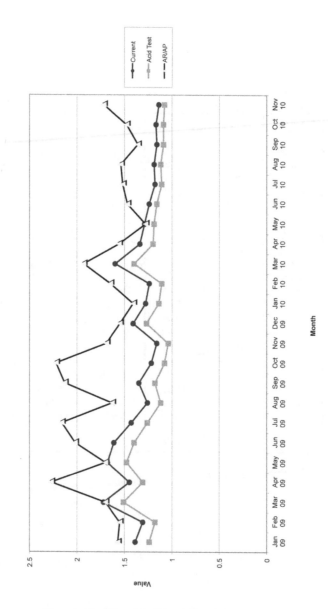

Figure 13. Monthly Liquidity Ratios

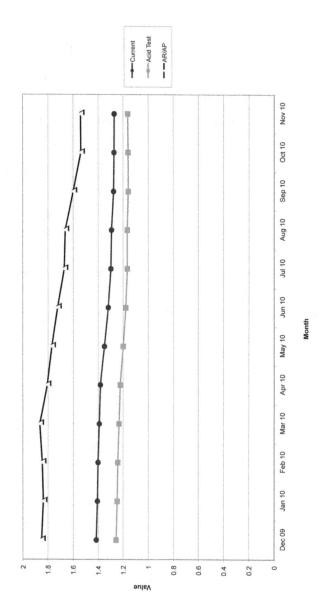

Figure 14. Trailing Liquidity Ratios

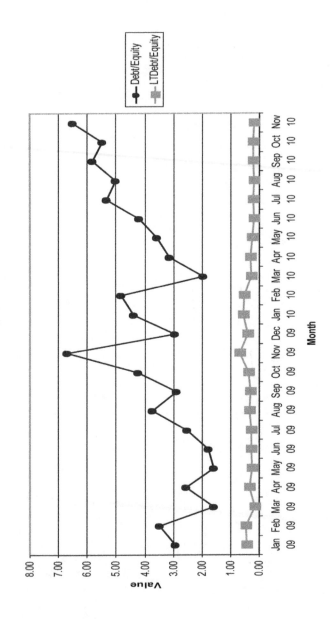

Figure 15. Monthly Debt Ratios

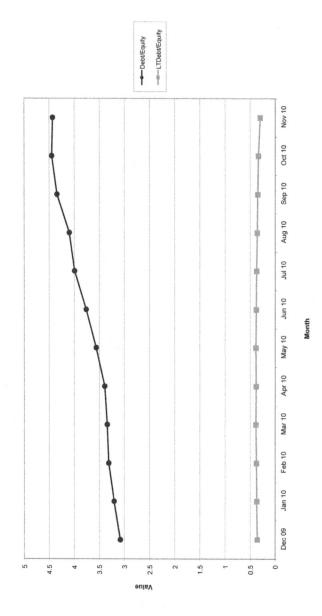

Figure 16. Trailing Debt Ratios

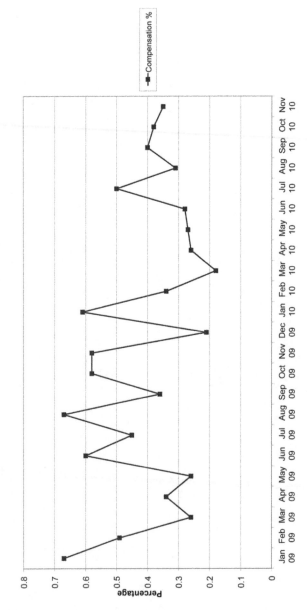

Figure 17. Monthly Percentage Compensation Ratios

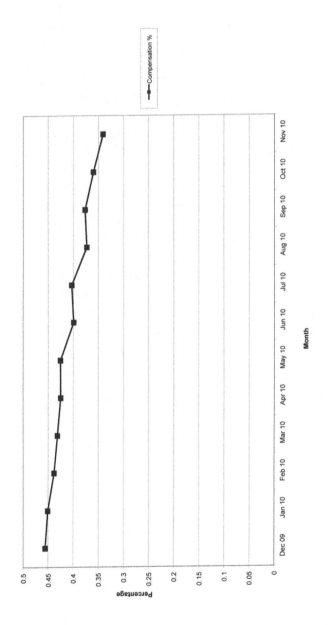

Figure 18. Trailing Percentage Compensation Ratios

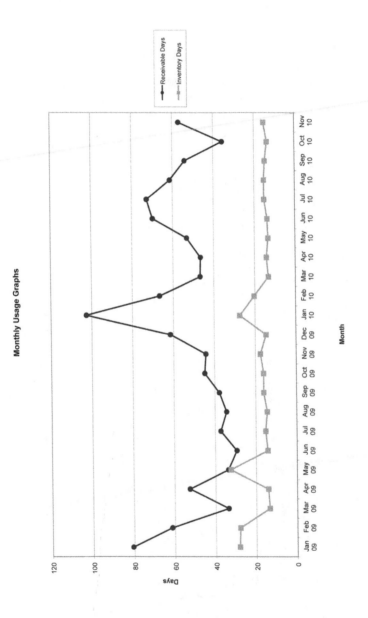

Figure 19. Monthly Receivable and Inventory Days Ratios

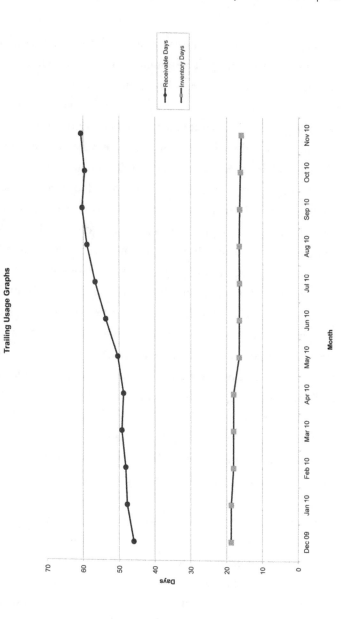

Figure 20. Trailing Receivable and Inventory Days Ratios

Figure 9 shows the current ratio, acid test, and accounts receivable to accounts payable monthly and trailing ratios. You can make sense out of what is happening with the company on a monthly basis as you look at the graphs of the data. When you look at Figure 13, you can see the seasonality of this business. The current ratio and the acid test increase and decrease as profitability increases and decreases during busy and slow months.

The current ratio and the acid test should also mirror each other, like they do in Figure 13. This means that the distance between the two graphs remains about equal. When this happens, your gross margin is consistent on a month-to-month basis. An increasing spread between the two ratios should be a warning sign. This means that inventory is increasing. Why is inventory increasing? If it is because of a pre-season purchase, then you should expect the spread to increase for a month or two. If employees are buying too much inventory in relationship to what the company is using to produce products and services, you'll see this buying spree, because the spread between the two ratios will increase.

The accounts receivable to accounts payable ratio also varies according to seasonality. This ratio is also covered with the receivable-days graph, because the receivable days impact this ratio.

Figure 14 shows the trailing data for each liquidity ratio. It tells a very alarming story for this company. Their trailing data shows that the company is becoming less profitable on a long-term basis (the current ratio and acid tests are decreasing, as is the accounts receivable to accounts payable ratio). This is not evident if you look only at the monthly liquidity ratios. That's why it's important to graph both monthly and trailing ratios.

Debt Ratio Trends

There are two ways to measure whether your company is too debt ridden. These are the debt-to-equity ratio and the long-term debt to equity ratio.

The debt-to-equity ratio looks at all debt, both current and long-term liabilities. The long-term debt to equity ratio looks only at long-term debt—those liabilities the companies owes for more than one year. These ratios are computed from your balance sheet each month.

Figure 15 shows the graph of the debt ratios. It's hard to see what is happening, because there are months where the debt-to-equity ratio is high, and months where it is low. The long-term debt to equity ratio is staying fairly constant.

Figure 16 shows the trailing data for each debt ratio. The trailing data gives a warning to the company owners. The company is adding a lot of short-term debt on a yearly basis.

The debt-to-equity ratio is increasing rapidly. If the company isn't starting many large projects, this means that it is rapidly buying materials and equipment. This should be a warning sign to watch purchase orders and other expenses. Make sure that you don't drain your cash reserves.

The long-term debt is staying constant on a trailing basis. Even though the company is not taking on long-term debt, it must closely watch cash to ensure that it can continue to pay its bills as it is taking on more debt.

Productivity or Percentage-Compensation Trends

Figure 17 shows the monthly graph of the percentage-compensation ratio. It's hard to see what is happening, because there are months where the ratio is as high as seventy percent, and other months where it is about twenty percent. This means in some months the company spends seventy cents of each dollar it brings in on payroll and payroll taxes. Other months it spends twenty cents of each dollar it generates on payroll and payroll taxes. The company has productive months and non-productive months. Or it is not tracking its labor consistently.

Figure 18 shows the trailing data graph for the percentage-compensation ratio.

The trailing data graph for this company shows a good story. The percentage-compensation ratio is decreasing on a long-term basis. This is good because it means that the company is becoming more productive each month.

If your company performs a lot of work that requires work-in-progress accounting, you'll need to add the work-in-progress estimated revenue from the balance sheet each month to the sales data on the profit and loss statement. Take the payroll and payroll taxes from the monthly payroll reports, rather than from the profit and loss statement. This will give you a truer value for your percentage-compensation ratio.

Percentage compensation should be constant on a long-term basis, since all seasonality is eliminated when you calculate the trailing data points. The companies with the lowest percentage compensation are usually the most profitable.

Usage Ratios: Inventory Days and Receivable Days Trends

The inventory days and receivable days are calculated from the inventory turns and receivable turns. The days trends are what you need to watch each month. If your company does not have inventory, you don't need to calculate inventory turns or days.

The receivable-days ratio must be looked at in conjunction with the accounts receivable to payable ratio. If the receivable-to-payables ratio is increasing and the receivable days are increasing too, then the company has a collection problem. If the receivable-to-payables ratio is increasing and the receivable days are constant, then the company is becoming more profitable. The reverse is also true: if the receivable-to-payable days are decreasing and the receivable days are constant, then the company is becoming less profitable.

Figure 19 shows the graph of the inventory and receivable ratios. Both the receivable days and inventory days increase and decrease each month. It's hard to see what is happening because there are months where the accounts receivable days are as high as one hundred and other months as low as thirty. The inventory days also range.

Figure 20 shows the trailing data points for the turns and days ratios.

The trailing data graph for this company shows a good story for inventory usage and a warning for receivable days. Inventory usage remains fairly constant on a long-term basis, which means that the company is being efficient with inventory. It is not building up inventory on a long-term basis.

However, the receivable days show a different story. The company has a collection problem. The fact that receivable days hit one hundred days during a month is definitely a warning sign that someone has to start calling overdue accounts. The long-term trend is still rising. Even though the receivable-to-payable ratio is decreasing, the company's receivable-days ratio is a warning sign to continue collection efforts. This ratio will eventually start decreasing on a long-term basis as the monthly receivable days start decreasing.

The last thing to look at is to make sure that the receivable days are higher than the inventory days, as they are with this company on a long-term analysis. This means that your company doesn't have too much inventory.

Have the courage to take thirty minutes each month to calculate the ten operating ratios and graph the monthly and long-term trends. This is critical to ensuring that your company can pay its bills, isn't carrying too much debt, doesn't have a collection problem, and is productive.

Chapter 10

Financial Fruit Salad
Is a Recipe for Disaster

One of the most critical elements to track on financial statements is the company's (or a department's) gross margin. It must be consistent from month to month. To calculate gross margin:

$$\text{Gross margin (GM)} = \frac{\text{Gross Profit}}{\text{Sales}}$$

Gross margin (GM) is always a percentage. Gross profit is always dollars. If your department's gross margin is supposed to be 45 percent, it must be 45 percent each month. One month at 45 percent, the next at 49 percent, and the following at 42 percent means that your gross margin is not consistent. It can vary by a percentage point or two around 45 percent, but no more.

Gross-profit dollars will vary each month. They depend on sales volume. Your gross margin should be constant. If your gross margin isn't constant from month to month, what is going on? There are six major reasons why your gross margin isn't consistent.

REASON #1: FRUIT SALAD IN
YOUR PROFIT AND LOSS STATEMENT.

This is the most prevalent reason, and it usually means that you have a lazy bookkeeper.

Financial fruit salad occurs when revenues do not match expenses incurred while producing those revenues each month. In one month, you have revenue—i.e., apples. The next month, you have expenses incurred producing those revenues—i.e., oranges. You have fruit salad! You don't want fruit salad. Revenues must match the costs of producing those revenues each month. You want apples matching apples. Or, if you like them better, bananas matching bananas. No mixtures; only the same fruit!

In the months that you have revenues and no expenses, your gross margins will be artificially high. In months that you have expenses and no revenues, your gross margins will be artificially low. You can't manage well and ensure your costs are not rising when you have fruit salad.

Fruit salad generally happens at the end of the month. The managers want to get in all the revenue for the month but don't necessarily care about all of the expenses. This is not a good idea. If you have department managers, they must focus on revenue *and* net operating profit. Too many companies track only sales and don't pay attention to costs. The revenue for all the work that got done in that month is usually accounted for in the month the work was done. Payroll issues generally force labor to be accounted for in the month it has incurred. However, the feeling is that the material and equipment expense aren't as important. There isn't the same immediacy as payroll, because you don't have to pay the vendors until the tenth of the following month. So the rush to close the month doesn't include all of the equipment and material expenses for that month. Fruit salad!

I've actually seen financial statements with gross margins ranging from a negative 6 percent to more than 50 percent over a few months. A swing of more than 56 percent. Your pricing rarely, if ever, changes 56 percent within a few months. You can't have a negative gross margin (in reality) unless you sell your products for less than the cost of labor, materials, equipment, etc. This isn't likely to happen in real life. When this happens, your bookkeeper is probably lazy and not paying attention.

You need accurate financial statements to manage properly. Make sure that your profit and loss statement doesn't have fruit salad. If you don't have financial statement fruit salad, then you have to look further to find the reason why you have inconsistent gross margins.

Reason #2: Inconsistent Pricing

The next place to look for inconsistent gross margins is pricing. Does one person in your company charge the customer more than another person? Or does one salesperson estimate low labor cost so he can get the projects? Here's Jeff's story:

Jeff's salesperson wanted to win all of the sales so that he received large commission checks. He was paid on the sale amount rather than the profit that the project realized. The salesperson didn't care about an accurate estimate. He cared about getting the project! Since the number of estimated hours were lower, the price to the customer was lower and the salesperson won most of his proposed work. However, as it turned out, the company lost, because the salesperson's proposed prices were lower than the cost to do the work, once overhead was figured into the project costs.

The field crews knew what was going on. They never said a word to me, but they joked about the estimated hours. The field crews came up with the phrase, "salesperson time versus field time." They knew that they could not perform the work in the estimated hours.

Jeff finally looked at the commission sheets and realized what the salesperson was doing. His salesperson's commission structure changed to being paid on profit rather than sales. Sales commissions were calculated AFTER the job was completed in the estimated hours. Prices to customers increased, and he lost a few jobs. However, now everyone was earning a profit—the salesperson and the company.

In addition to salesperson time, look at bids versus actual costs. If a salesperson bid 12 hours on a project and the job took 16 hours, then your gross margin will be lower than projected. On the positive side, if a salesperson bid 12 hours and the project took 10 hours, then you have a higher gross margin than projected. Either way, the gross margin won't be consistent with the bid.

REASON #3: WARRANTY EXPENSES

This occurs when you complete a project and something fails within the time period that your company guarantees workmanship. You have additional expense with no revenues against those expenses. In the case of warranty, you may recover part of the expense if you can submit warranty claims to suppliers. This is costly in terms of profits and customer satisfaction, because you have an unhappy customer and a negative gross profit each time your company has warranty expense.

REASON #4: PAYING EMPLOYEES OVERTIME AND CHARGING THE CUSTOMER REGULAR TIME

There may be projects that your company performs on a fixed price. Sometimes, to complete the project on time, you pay your employees overtime. Expenses increase for the same selling price. This means gross margin decreases. Or your company promises no overtime costs to its best customers. If that customer needs your company's services during "non-normal" hours (i.e., weekends and evenings), you may pay your employees overtime to take care of those customers, even though those customers don't pay overtime costs.

In either case, the gross margin decreases, because you are paying your employees overtime, and you are charging the customer regular rates rather than overtime rates. You still have the same selling price to the customer. Yes, you can be busy and be less profitable, because your margins are lower!

REASON #5: EXPENSING INVENTORY (FOR COMPANIES THAT HAVE INVENTORY)

You place a large inventory order. When the order comes in, the bookkeeping department expenses that material (i.e., puts the inventory cost in direct expense on your P&L rather than inventory on your balance sheet). When you order materials for future use, it is inventory until you need it for a product. Once that inventory is used, it is taken out of inventory and put in direct cost. You always need a revenue to offset the materials expense.

Reason #6: Theft

If reasons 1 through 5 are not the reason why you have inconsistent gross margins, then the likelihood is that employees are stealing materials. Theft is often a surprise to owners. However, have the courage to investigate if you suspect a theft problem. Theft is usually discovered during inventory counts, when the actual inventory is much less than what it is supposed to be based on the balance-sheet value. Hopefully, this is not the case in your company.

Here is Gary's story:

> Gary knew his company financial statements very well. He was confident that he knew job costs and that all of the revenues and expenses were accounted for in the same month. The company's gross margin started dropping. Not by a lot, but by a percentage or two every month. This was puzzling. In addition, material purchases started going up. Again, not by much; by a little every month.
>
> The only explanation for this was theft. Gary didn't want to believe it and didn't do anything about the lower gross margins for about six months. He had cameras in parts of the warehouse, which didn't show anyone was stealing, so he thought that everything was okay.
>
> After being told again and again that he had a theft problem, Gary finally started an investigation. One weekend

he finally put a camera in the warehouse where there hadn't been one before. Gary saw materials going out. He also noticed that the fence was cut. It was subtle, so you couldn't immediately see the cuts as you were driving by. But it was open to facilitate the removal of inventory. Gary caught the thief and prosecuted him.

Watch your gross margins each month. Ensure they stay constant. If not, these six frequent occurrences should give you where to look for the issues. Have the courage to fix the issues.

Chapter 11

Inventory Is a Bet

I f you have inventory, make sure you count it.

Not all businesses have inventory. If your company produces products for sale, then you have inventory. You use your hard-earned cash to purchase parts and pieces that you think you will be able to sell. You are betting your cash on your ability to forecast sales.

Over the years, I've seen thousands of dollars in warehouses gathering dust. Your supplier had a great sale. You bought the parts because they were "cheap." You paid for the "cheap parts." Unfortunately, after a few months, you realize you bought too many parts, because the ones you didn't use sat on the shelf for years, gathering dust. The supplier won, because he sold the company the parts, which the company paid for. The company lost, because you spent money on the parts and didn't use them.

You bet your hard-earned cash, and you lost. Inventory is a bet. Here is Jack's story:

Jack took over the company from his father. His father was a "pack rat." Jack was also a pack rat. Inventory was overflowing. It was everywhere in his warehouse. No one accounted for parts, pieces, and tools. They couldn't bear to dispose of any obsolete inventory. Someone, somewhere, sometime might need it. No one knew where all of the company tools were. Employees took whatever they thought they needed to produce their jobs. No one tracked what was taken.

It took almost nine months to convince Jack to lock up the warehouse. I made him a deal: he could have a small space in the warehouse for any inventory that he couldn't bear to part with. This obsolete inventory area would not be counted as part of the inventory.

One Saturday, Jack got the courage to lock up the warehouse and put the inventory in its proper place so it could easily be tracked. They disposed of six dumpsters full of obsolete parts and built the walls and gating they needed to lock up the warehouse.

What happened? Jack's company saw an immediate increase in cash flow, because they weren't buying inventory they already had. In addition, tools didn't have to be replaced, because they were tracked and didn't "disappear."

Uncontrolled warehouses are a great drain of cash, as is not counting inventory. Have the courage to take the time to count inventory at least once per year.

Here's Chuck's story:

> *Chuck ran a multimillion-dollar business that was heavily dependent on inventory. There were approximately thirty-five people who touched inventory every day so that Chuck's company could provide the equipment and services to its clients.*
>
> *The balance sheet said there was over $500,000 in inventory in the building. This figure didn't change from month to month. The company hadn't done a physical count in more than two years. After several months of prodding, the company finally took the time to count the inventory. It was less than $250,000. The company lost a quarter of a million dollars in net worth in one day! (Inventory losses go directly against the profits on your profit and loss statement. Additional parts were used but never accounted for.)*

How easy was this to happen? A $250,000 loss in two years is $125,000 per year. Divide $125,000 by 52 weeks, and the loss per week is $2,403 per week, or $481 per day, or $14 per person per day.

With the value of the inventory at Chuck's company, $14 represented a fraction of the value of one part.

Have the courage to lock up your warehouses, count your inventory on a yearly basis, and do something about inventory losses!

Chapter 12

Growth Masks Unprofitability

If you operate your business on a cash basis, or you don't pay attention to your financial statements as the company grows, your company can be unprofitable and still survive.

Here's Fred's story:

> *Fred started a company with a partner. They were very good at what they did, and the work started flowing in. They hired employees and trained them well. The company had a great reputation for doing quality work, and the company grew.*
>
> *Fred didn't pay attention to the company financial statements. The CPA was supposed to do that. The CPA asked questions about inventory and job costs. Fred guessed, since they didn't have time to delve into those unimportant things. The company profit and loss statement, provided to them*

by their CPA using the figures they gave him, showed that the company was profitable. The CPA never questioned the information that was given to him to compile their financial statements and taxes.

Fred's thought: the company was growing, and we need to pay attention to customers. As long as we had the cash to do what we wanted to do and all of the bills were paid, we were doing great.

The company grew to about $2,000,000 in revenues and stopped growing. They were stable at that level of sales and comfortable with managing the number of employees needed to produce that $2,000,000. They started noticing that it became harder and harder to pay all of the bills. They didn't have the cash flow that they used to have. Something was wrong.

I analyzed Fred's operations. At the end of the analysis, I showed them that once overhead was taken into consideration, the company was losing five cents for every dollar it took in the door.

How could that be? They guessed at inventory. They gave a number to the CPA each year to include on their taxes without actually counting it. They had no clue about material shrinkage and job cost. That was their undoing. These guesses were what caused the profit and loss statement to have a positive bottom line rather than showing a loss.

Growth masked many problems. The cash from one project started the next project. As long as the company was growing, there was sufficient cash collected to pay the bills from that project and start the next project. Since the loss was "only a nickel," when they stopped growing, it took a while to

start seeing that the company was having problems paying its
bills. The growth hid the cash shortages.

Fred was smart to get help and lucky that the company had a great reputation. He was able to raise the company's prices to cover the shortfall. Several of their customers also remarked that they could never understand how the company could provide quality work as cheap as they had been doing it!

Having cash does not mean that you are profitable. Pay attention to knowing what your costs are to truly understand whether your company is profitable.

Stage Three

TAKE ACTION
BASED ON YOUR
FINANCIAL REVIEW

Chapter 13

I Understand My Financial Statements—Now What?

Congratulations! You're receiving accurate cash-flow information every week and timely, accurate financial statements every month.

You can analyze your financial statements, or you can do nothing. The choice is yours. Communicate the results with your employees and advisors. The communication will be different based on what your statements are telling you.

Have the courage to communicate the good and the bad.

The reality is that your employees know when "things are good" and when "things are bad." They watch your movements, your attitude, your communication, and how you do what you do. The nonverbal clues that you give in good times and bad times are louder than the words you say.

It's much better to communicate verbally, so that the rumor mill doesn't run rampant, and before you know it, a minor issue has the company going out of business.

Assuming that you've written your three-page business plan (chapter 16) and all of your employees had input into the goals, they want to see what the results are. They will also have suggestions for you when things aren't going according to plan.

Here's Michael's story:

> Michael is the second-generation owner of his company. His father-in-law started the tradition of meeting with the employees the first Friday of every year. Now that he is retired, Michael has continued this tradition and enjoys this "State-of-the-Company" breakfast meeting each year.
>
> During the breakfast, which is held off-site, he discusses how the company did compared to the previous year's goals and budget. All of the company's 75+ employees have input into the goal-setting process. During the meeting, Michael also reveals the plans for the next five years. That's right—five years. He feels it is important to look at industry trends for more than one year, so the company can be prepared to take advantage of opportunities.
>
> When he looks back on all of the years of planning, it's very rare that Michael's company doesn't meet yearly goals. Each of the department managers is responsible for meeting with his or her department each month to discuss where that department is in relation to the goals for that department. When economic times are tough, as they have been, it's the employees who come up with the ideas to increase revenues

and cut costs. In good times and bad, the company almost always makes their goals.

It's also comforting to Michael to know that he doesn't have to come up with all of the ideas when the company is having problems. Either the managers or Michael explains the issue and asks for help. Employees know that their ideas are appreciated and often implemented. It's much better to have 75+ heads working on a problem rather than Michael's alone!

During your reviews, if you see a problem with the cash-flow reports, then start digging immediately. Don't wait for a monthly meeting. Cash is the lifeblood of your business. Get back up for the numbers. Look at the deposit slips, the accounts receivable aging reports, and the accounts payable aging reports. Find out quickly why you are having a cash problem.

From a monthly reporting perspective, the first thing is to schedule the thirty minutes on your calendar to review the financial statements each month. Then look at the ratios and the trend analyses. A minor issue, when spotted early, can be resolved before it causes major problems. If you don't take action, that minor issue will probably not go away. It will get worse! Do something about it before it becomes a major problem, and you are diverted from normal business operations and thrown into survival mode.

What's the worst that could happen?

- A valued employee could leave. If the rumor mill starts something false, that employee might get scared and leave anyway. Communication takes care of the rumor mill.

- You could run out of cash if you don't take action. That *will* kill your business.
- A valued customer could stop doing business with your company. As long as you have cultivated many customers, the loss of a customer, while sad, won't kill your business. Learn from the reason why that customer left and don't make a similar mistake.
- You can get angry and let your emotions rule.

"WHEN YOU BECOME ANGRY, YOU BECOME STUPID"

Actually, I wish that I had said that, because it sums up what I've always believed and taught: you can't make rational decisions when you are emotional.

"When you become angry, you become stupid," said Dr. Ned Hallowell on the May 2012 Success Magazine audio CD. He feels, as I do, that to make good decisions, you have to get emotion out of the decision.

When you first find the alarming things that your financial statements are telling you, you might not believe them, you might get angry, or you may feel like you've been kicked in the stomach. If you find someone has been stealing from you, your initial emotions totally overtake your rational thought process. If one of your employees does something totally stupid, you get angry.

My rule has always been to never fire someone when you are mad or upset. If it's the right thing to do when you are mad, it will be the right thing to do the next morning when you are calmer.

You've got to get rid of the emotion to make rational decisions. For some people, getting rid of the emotion takes minutes. For others, it may take days or even weeks. The key is to get rid of the emotion as quickly as possible, so you can take the steps necessary to resolve the issue before it blows up into a major crisis.

In my first book, *The Ugly Truth about Small Business*, every business owner I interviewed went through horrible business situations and survived. The initial reaction to the event, for everyone, was emotional rather than rational. Each person dealt with it in their own way. Dr. Hallowell suggests that you do seventy-five jumping jacks, run up and down stairs, or do some other strong physical exercise for three minutes. You'll feel better.

As a runner, I've gotten some of my best ideas on long runs. And if I'm totally stressed out, there is nothing like running hard for forty-five minutes to make me feel better. And yes, I usually don't want to get on the treadmill to start. However, usually ten to fifteen minutes into the run, I'm already feeling better.

I've given dispatchers, the people in contracting companies who are responsible for taking customers' calls and scheduling technicians, red styrofoam bricks for years. (These are similar to the Nerf balls that we used as kids.) Dispatchers have the most stressful job in a contracting company. You can throw the bricks at something and not hurt it most of the time. You can squeeze them, and you can do crazy things to make you laugh. The point is to laugh. You can't be mad and laugh at the same time.

I don't mean to suggest that an angry customer or technician is as devastating as some business problems. However, the idea is the same—getting rid of the emotional stress is critical to being able to function rationally.

At some point, logic and rational thinking begin to emerge. This is when you can plan and when you get the good ideas to resolve the situation. You begin dealing with the fear and the unknown.

Get rid of the emotion (anger) and get rational as quickly as possible. It's better for your employees, you, and your company's profitability.

My philosophy has always been that there are many learning experiences. When things happen, they happen for a reason. Figure out what went wrong, fix it, and don't make the same mistake again. The only time you fail is when you don't learn from your mistakes and make the same ones over again.

Spot the minor issues before they become major crises, and have the courage to take care of them.

Chapter 14

You Can Delegate, but You Can't Abdicate

Usually the first person a company owner hires is a bookkeeper. The owner breathes a sigh of relief. "Accounting is now taken care of." You can delegate the responsibility for the bookkeeping, but you still have overall responsibility for the results.

Here is Jane's story:

Jane is a florist. She hired a bookkeeping firm to prepare her financial statements. She got her financial statements at the end of each month, looked at the bottom line, and saw that she had a profit. She put the statements in the drawer and forgot about them. Jane made a mistake that many business owners do—trusting financial statements without looking at them.

Jane began having problems paying her bills. This puzzled her, because her financial statements showed that she was profitable each month. She called me. I looked at the statements, asked a few questions, and got a blank stare and silence back. I said, "You really don't know how to read these, do you?" She admitted that she didn't. I wrote a list of questions to ask the bookkeeping service. It turned out that whenever they didn't know where something belonged, they put it in miscellaneous sales! This inflated her sales, and as a result she had inaccurate, unreliable financial statements.

Jane fired them. I made her take a bookkeeping course, where she said she spent the three most miserable months of her life. However, now she knew enough to question a statement that didn't look right. She still delegated the creation of the financial statements, but she didn't abdicate the responsibility for reviewing the statements and the results.

You can delegate the day-to-day bookkeeping operations and creation of the financial statements. However, you cannot abdicate the responsibility for those results. You still must require timely, accurate monthly financial statements. You must invest the thirty minutes reviewing the financial statements and adding to your trend analyses.

Have the courage to review the statements, react to what they are telling you, and implement procedures to take care of the negative situations that you see.

Chapter 15

Watch Your Cash

Cash is the lifeblood of a business. With it, business owners can survive and thrive. Without it, the business dies.

For a business to profitably survive, cash must be properly accounted for and managed. You must be able to trust the people who handle your cash.

Over the past more than thirty years I've seen a lot of embezzlement from companies by employees. Of the people who work for you, 99.9 percent are honest. The 0.1 percent come to your business to embezzle. A very wise person once told me, "The job of a good embezzler is to become the trusted bookkeeper." No matter what safeguards you put in place, this person is going to find a way to steal from you.

What about the other 99.9 percent? They or a family member get in trouble (sickness, death, divorce, etc.), and they need money. However, when faced with stressful situations, they may do things that are morally and ethically wrong because they aren't thinking straight. If you don't have systems in place, they get tempted and may try. Once they find they aren't caught, the second time it becomes easier—the third time even easier. Before you know it, they've taken thousands of dollars. They know it isn't right, but their emotional needs override their values system. When they don't get caught, they continue. By putting the separation-of-duties procedures in place, you send a message that makes it very difficult for the honest people to do something stupid.

Here is Arnold's story:

Arnold had a competent bookkeeper. She produced accurate and timely financial statements. After about three years working for the company, she went through a horrible divorce. The lawyer told her that if he didn't receive $3,000 within a week, he was dropping her case. What did she do? She forged a check to pay him. She thought that since she received the bank statements, she could easily pull the check from the statements, and no one would find them.

Luckily Arnold's banker was reviewing the company's account and happened to see the check she had forged to the attorney. The banker called him and asked, "Do you know lawyer X?" Arnold didn't know lawyer X and asked him why he asked the question.

The banker told him that he had a check written to lawyer X on the company's account, and the signature looked different.

Arnold raced to the bank. He found the forged check and confronted the bookkeeper, who confessed.

He said to her, "Why didn't you come to us? You know we loan our employees money, because you take the repayments out of their payroll checks each week!"

She wasn't thinking rationally because of the emotional situation. It turned out that she had forged a total of $6,000 to the attorney.

Arnold prosecuted her, and she went to jail. Had she been thinking rationally rather than emotionally, she would have come to them, because she knew that the company loaned money to employees!

Arnold was smart in one area. He didn't give their bookkeeper check signing authority. Had he done so, he couldn't have prosecuted her criminally. The judge would have said that she had check-signing authority, so she could write any check.

The other thing that would have prevented this was if the company bank statements were sent to the owner's home. Arnold would have reviewed the statement and seen the forged check. In this case, she would have known he would have seen the checks (or today, seen the pictures of the checks) and probably not have forged the checks.

Follow these actions, and you'll have a better chance of keeping the honest people honest—and potentially save yourself thousands of your hard-earned dollars.

Here are twenty procedures you should implement to keep the honest people honest.

1. Send your bank statements home.

The most important thing you *must* do is to have your bank statements sent to your home. Go through the checks every month. You'll learn a lot. In addition, you'll learn about checks that have bounced, learn about late loan payments, and be the first to get the bank correspondence concerning your hard-earned money. This is the first line of defense in making sure that you keep the honest people honest when they are dealing with *your* money.

It takes no more than fifteen minutes to go through the statement. Look at who the checks are written to and the signatures on the checks. Ask questions when there is a check written to someone or a company you don't recognize. This is sending a message to your bookkeeper.

"But," you say, "I get my bank statement in my office unopened." My answer is: the envelope still can be steamed open. In addition, even if you get the statements in the office "unopened," you still may not get the notices of bounced checks, late payments, and other bank correspondence about your account.

It might not always be your employees who are stealing. Here's Albert's story:

> Albert was looking through his bank statement and noticed that a check written to one of his vendors looked very high. The next morning, he took the bank statement to his bookkeeper and showed her the check picture. She pulled the check stub and original invoice. The check that the company wrote for $54 was changed to $554! One of his vendor's employees was stealing from him. Albert called the vendor and the bank. The company's $500 was refunded by the vendor.

2. GET YOUR FINANCIAL STATEMENTS ON TIME.

Your financial statements should be completed by the fifteenth of the following month. Look at them, calculate the ratios, do the long-term analyses, and understand what they are telling you. Have the courage to take action where you see problems.

Receiving January's results in March does you no good. Any minor issue that could have been dealt with might become a major crisis. Your financial statements are your scorecard. You need to know where you stand quickly.

3. DON'T ACCEPT EXCUSES FROM YOUR BOOKKEEPER.

Good bookkeepers are proud of producing timely, accurate financial statements. They are mortified if someone finds a mistake they've made in the preparation of your monthly P&L and balance sheet.

If your bookkeeper always has an excuse about the financial statements, you need to take a hard look at what is going on. That person may have reasons for burying "mistakes" to hide her embezzlement. If a software problem is truly causing the statements to be late, fix the problem! Not getting a financial statement and not balancing the checkbook are the two greatest warning signs that something is amiss.

4. QUESTION SUDDEN CHANGES IN GROSS MARGINS.

One of the easiest ways to steal from your company is to order materials from your suppliers on your accounts and send them to a company that the person ordering the materials owns. Your company has additional expenses that you don't question, because the expenses are from your vendors. You just sign the checks. The person ordering has no materials expense and makes a great profit for his company.

The easiest way to catch this is through watching your gross margins each month. If your gross margins go down, you need to know why. With no explanation, there is a great likelihood that materials are "walking out of your company" because of a dishonest employee.

Each month balance inventory and cost of goods sold. The formula is: beginning inventory plus purchases minus ending inventory equals cost of goods sold. If it doesn't, then find out why. Things may be "walking out the back door."

5. IF CASH OR A CHECK IS GIVEN AS PAYMENT, THE PERSON RECEIVING THE PAYMENT NOTES THAT HE OR SHE HAS RECEIVED IT ON AN INVOICE.

Here's Michael's story:

> *Michael noticed a check flying around in the wind in the parking lot of his company. He picked up the check and saw that it was written to the company for payment for work that was done. Michael didn't say anything about the check. He just put the check in his desk drawer to see what would happen.*
>
> *A few days later the bookkeeper came to him and said that a technician had told her that the customer had paid by check and that he didn't have the check any more. However, the check wasn't attached to the service ticket when the bookkeeper got it. The bookkeeper didn't want to accuse the technician of lying and didn't want to call the*

*customer to make sure she had paid, since this would look
bad for the company.*

*Michael pulled the check out of his drawer and was
relieved that the bookkeeper was honest enough to come to
him with the issue. From that day forward, staplers were
issued, and all checks and cash were stapled to the invoices.*

This situation could have been avoided with a sign-off policy.
When an employee signs off that she has received cash or the
check, then there is no question about the last person responsible
for that payment. If the bookkeeper had been required to sign off
that she had received that check, the missing check would have
been noticed with the employee standing there, and the situation
could have been resolved at that time.

The person receiving the cash from the customer, or another
employee who has been paid by the customer, signs off that he
or she has received the cash. This lets you see the flow of checks
and cash from the customer to the employee to the office. Then
the customer or the employee is "off the hook," because there is
written documentation that the money was turned in.

6. CHECK YOUR DEPOSITS ON THE BANK STATEMENT AGAINST THE DEPOSIT SLIPS.

Here's Martha's story:

*Martha owns a retail shop. The store receives cash,
checks, and credit cards for payment. Her former bookkeeper
went to the bank every day with the deposits. Unbeknownst
to Martha, she changed the deposit slips so that only the*

checks, credit card slips, and most of the cash were deposited. She pocketed a few dollars every week.

It took about six months to find this out, because the company's financials were not in good shape either. The bookkeeper was simply changing the deposit slips and changing the books to reflect the lower sales.

Martha caught her one week because the store had large cash deposits, and she started adding the sales up in her head. The books didn't match the deposits. Martha started digging and found the embezzlement.

Make sure there is a receipt that lists the deposits singly. You'll see the cash and the checks. The other thing to do is to make a copy of all of the checks and cash that are deposited with the deposit slip. Then there are no questions about differences in deposits. Sometimes the bank makes a mistake and loses a check. If you have copies of all of the checks and cash that you deposited, then there are no questions.

7. Do not accept a postdated check.

In most states, if you accept a postdated check and the check bounces, when you go to court to collect, all the writer of the check has to do is to go to the judge and say that you knowingly accepted a check without sufficient funds. Case dismissed. You're out hundreds or thousands of dollars.

If you write a check in a supermarket and put the wrong date on it, most times the clerk will ask you to put the right date on it. This is the reason why.

So, what do you do? Ask your customer to put the date the work is done or the date that you are collecting for the work on the check. You can choose to hold it for a few days to ensure that it clears. However, the date you actually received the check must be on it.

8. Print out a list of your vendors every quarter.

Make sure that you know who all of your vendors are. Print out a vendor list yourself. If you don't know how to print out the list, ask the bookkeeper to do it while you watch. Look at the names on the list. Notice if there are two similar names. Ask questions. You'll avoid duplicate payments and checks to, for example, ABC Business and ABC Industries. It's very easy to open a checking account with a similar name to a vendor with whom you do a lot of business. Just a few hundred dollars per month in this bogus account adds up to a lot of money over the years.

9. The person who balances the checkbook does not sign checks.

Unless you the owner are balancing the checkbook, the person balancing the checkbook should not have check-signing authority. Arnold's story at the beginning of this chapter illustrates this point.

10. Make sure you see the confirmation number or deposit slips for payroll tax deposits.

You are ultimately responsible for the payment of these taxes. Make sure that they get paid. Ask to see the confirmation slips or bank deposit slips.

Here's why: A husband and wife own a company together. The wife does not have check-signing privileges. This husband and wife decide to get a divorce. The wife decides that she is going to "get my husband" and doesn't pay payroll taxes for a year. She got him!

**11. Stamp checks immediately with "for deposit only"
and the account number as soon as you get the checks.**
If the checks have "for deposit only" without an account number
stamped on them, it is very easy to put any checking account
number under it. If the checks have "for deposit only" with the
checking account number on them, it is much harder to put
them in an account that is not yours. In addition, if the checks
are left out and someone tries to steal the checks, it is much
more difficult to cash those checks with an account number
on them.

A bookkeeper who has been making your deposits for years
and knows everyone at the bank won't be questioned if she says,
"John wants me to open another account." She opens it in the
company's name, with her as the signatory on the account. It's
that easy.

12. Question changes in behavior and start digging.
Find out the reason for any change in behavior you notice in your
bookkeeper or any other employee who touches cash. For example,
if your bookkeeper starts becoming very withdrawn, or you find
out that a major crisis has occurred in her family, start checking
very closely. Mistakes may become more frequent, because she isn't
paying attention to what is going on due to her personal life. If
this happens, then you need to constantly check on her work. She
might need time off to "get her head together," so that the books
are accurate again.

This is the time where emotions can override values and
ethics. Make sure you have all of your cash procedures and
separation of duties in place. She will be less likely to be stealing
from your company.

13. WATCH SCANNER USE IN YOUR BUSINESS.

Scanners can be used for many legitimate things: entering logos into a computer, entering documents quickly into a computer, etc. However, they can also be used for illegal activities, such as scanning a check with your signature on it into a computer.

An employee took one of his payroll checks and scanned it into the computer. With a little clean up, he had a great signature, which he put on company checks that he wrote to himself and other companies he set up. He was caught $96,000 later. The bank did nothing, because there was a legal signature on the check—after all, it was the owner's signature!

How did he get the checks? He'd steal one from near the top of the box of checks. No one questioned an out-of-sequence check. Or, by the time the bank statement came in, that check was in sequence.

14. MATCH ACCOUNTS PAYABLE AND ACCOUNTS RECEIVABLE LISTS WITH THE TOTAL ON YOUR BALANCE SHEET.

Make sure that the list of payables and receivables that you print out match the totals on your balance sheet. If they don't match, find out why. Someone may be adjusting payables or receivables on the balance sheet and paying the cash to himself with a counter check from the bank or a manual check, rather than a computer check.

15. HAVE A WEEKLY CASH-FLOW REPORT ON YOUR DESK BY 5 P.M. EACH FRIDAY.

A weekly cash-flow report delineates what has happened with your business each week. You'll know what deposits came in, what checks were written, and have an estimate of the cash needed the following week. (See chapter 9 for the cash-flow report form). Keep these forms so you can refer to them from year to year. You will have a good idea of the company's cash flow on a weekly, monthly, and yearly basis.

16. No signature stamps.

Even if two signatures are required on checks, if you have a signature stamp, one of the signatures could be that stamp. It makes it easy to write a check to pay personal bills on the company account. For example, one of the authorized signers on your checking account could easily pay the corporate American Express bill and his personal American Express bill. Others wouldn't notice it if one of the signatures just happened to be a signature stamp.

One of the worst things that I ever had to do as part of my business consulting activities was to tell two partners of a three-partner company that the third partner was embezzling $50,000 per year from the company. And it was probably more. I quit searching at $50,000, because I felt sick. He did this using a signature stamp for one of the two required signatures. Since he balanced the checkbook, the other partners never knew.

17. Watch petty cash.

Petty cash must be balanced each week. If there is supposed to be $200 cash in petty cash, the total receipts and cash should add to $200 each week. When you sign a check to replace petty cash, ask for the receipts and check them. Again, it is easy to have a receipt from an office-supply company for a personal item. Ask questions.

This is one of the easiest places to take $10 or $20 per week that I've seen. Over ten years, this adds up to a lot of cash.

18. DON'T BE PREDICTABLE WITH RESPECT TO CASH.

If your company always disburses cash to employees for their out-of-town expenses on Monday mornings, then do it on a Friday afternoon once in a while. A business owner had many jobs out of town. The employees left on Monday mornings after meeting with the supervisors to discuss the week's work. The supervisors gave the employees their weekly expense money at those meetings. Word got out, and one day there was a robbery of all that cash very early that Monday morning, because someone knew it would be there.

19. LOCK UP YOUR CHECKS.

Whenever you are not printing the checks to pay invoices, they should be kept in a locked filing cabinet. This prevents an employee walking into an office and taking a check, or an outsider coming in and taking a group of checks from the bottom of the check stack.

20. WATCH CAREFULLY ALL THE TIME.

It's your hard-earned money. If you watch all of the time, understand how to read your financial statements, and ask questions a lot, you'll have a better chance of keeping the honest people honest. Trust no one with your money—okay, maybe your significant other. If you put these systems in place, you'll have the checks and balances you need to sleep more comfortably at night. However, when that little voice in the back of your head says that something isn't right, it probably isn't. Check out what is going on and ask questions. After all, it's your money that you're protecting.

If you find someone stealing from your company, have the courage to confront the embezzler and put that person in jail. Too many people fire the person and don't report it. Then that person does that same thing to another unsuspecting business owner.

Chapter 16

Easy Planning and Budgeting

Part of your financial statement review each month is seeing where the company and its departments are with respect to the budget.

Don't have a budget? You're like the millions of business owners who fly by the seat of their pants. Have the courage to plan once per year and work your plan.

Planning doesn't have to be an onerous six-month process. It can be fun, especially when you involve your employees in the goal-setting process. Once the goals are set, they will be curious as to the progress. You'll be forced to implement and report back.

If you have no employees, rely on an advisory board or a coach to keep you focused and implementing your plan.

Write an easy, simple three-page business plan. Do this for projects as well as the overall business each year. Use it every day, week, and month. It's not thirty pages. It doesn't sit on a shelf or in a drawer, never to be seen again. It's a practical tool that helps you implement what you say you want to do.

It takes some time to gather the information for those three pages. The three pages are a living, breathing document that you can put up on a wall to constantly remind you about where you want to go, and how you are doing achieving those goals.

Important! The business plan described on the next pages is an operational business plan. It is a breathing document that you look at every day. This business plan is *not* used if you need bank or venture-capital financing. It can form the basis for the business plan that a banker or investor requires. However, each of the pages needs to be described in much greater detail for a banker or investor.

As Dwight Eisenhower (and others) have said, "Failing to plan is planning to fail."

In reality, you plan all the time. However, it is planning for the "trees," or the operational side of your business, rather than the "forest," which is your overall business. For example, when a customer accepts your proposal or walks into your store, you usually follow a specific process, whether or not it is written down.

For a project it might go something like this: Salesperson meets with the customer, determines the customer's needs, and writes a proposal. The customer accepts the proposal. You create a job number, gather the materials necessary, and perform the work. The customer receives the work. You bill for the completed work, or the customer pays COD on completion.

If you plan your work, you can easily plan your business. Here are three easy pieces of paper that form your operational business plan: goals, marketing flow chart, and financial budget.

PAGE 1: GOALS

Have the courage to take a hard, realistic look at your business. What is really happening? Many times the owner of the business is the last to know when something is happening. Maybe a key employee is unhappy and looking for a job, or a project is not meeting budget, or there is another issue that is being "kept from the boss." When you start looking for what you want to accomplish, make sure that you get out of your office and talk to employees "on their turf" (in their offices, in the field, etc.), as well as customers at their locations or on the phone.

You want input from your employees when you set the company goals. If you set the goals alone, then they are your goals. Employees may or may not buy in. They may not help implement the goals because they have no interest in them.

However, when you include employees in the process, they have an interest in seeing the results because they had input. They are happy to work harder to ensure the goals are reached and to provide ideas if implementation is not going as planned.

Here is the goal-setting process with employees:

- Ask the goal-setting questions
- Gather their answers
- Report results
- Cull the goals list
- Publish the goals for the year

There are two different sets of questions: one for managers and one for non-managers. Put a notice in everyone's paychecks with the goal-setting questions and a due date. Answers can be anonymous. Designate someone to receive the sealed questionnaires.

Managerial questions to ask:

- What went right this year? How would you make sure that we continue doing the right things right?
- What went wrong this year? How would you do different things next year so that the same issues/problems don't arise?
- What works well in your department?
- What doesn't work well and how would you fix it?
- Do you think the different departments communicate well? If not, how would you fix the issues?
- What do you like about working here?
- What would you change?
- Did you see any new competitors coming into the market? If so, who?
- Did you see any existing competitors go out of business? If so, who?
- How many active customers do you have? How many inactive customers do you have that are less than five years old? (An inactive customer is one who has used your company's services in the past but has not used them in the past eighteen months.)
- How many active customers do you want next year?
- Are you satisfied with the personnel who work for you? If not, what are you going to do about it?
- What training needs does your team have?
- What did your competition do this year? Are they getting stronger? Weaker? Are you losing more or less work to them?

Here are the non-managerial employee questions:

- What went right this year? How would you make sure that we continue doing the right things right?
- What went wrong this year? How would you do different things next year so that the same issues/ problems don't arise?
- What works well in your department?
- What doesn't work well and how would you fix it?
- Do you think the different departments communicate well? If not, how would you fix the issues?
- What do you like about working here?
- What would you change?
- Did you see any new competitors coming into the market? If so, who?
- Did you see any existing competitors go out of business? If so, who?

Your goals should include sales goals, mix-of-business goals, number-of-customer goals, gross-margin goals, net-profit goals, and personal-income goals (which you don't have to share with your employees).

Your goals must be specific, measurable, and time oriented. For example, increasing the number of customers is a wish, not a goal. Increasing the number of customers from 550 to 1,000 by December 31, 20XX is a goal.

Once you have determined the goals with your employees, put them where everyone can see them. If the goal is "at the top of the stairs," you have to determine the stair steps, or objectives, to achieve the goals. Break the goals down into monthly objectives. Put the objectives somewhere you can see them and review them each month. Check off each objective as you complete it.

Page 2: Marketing

After establishing overall goals, or perhaps to help establish overall goals, study the source of your revenues—i.e., your customers. First, how many active customers do you have? An active customer is a customer who has used your company's products and services in the past eighteen months. How many inactive customers do you have? An inactive customer has used your company, but not in the past eighteen months to five years. Stop counting after five years. Most of the customers who haven't bought from your company in more than five years have moved (physically) or have used another company because you didn't keep in touch with them!

Call a random sample of your inactive customers. Find out why they haven't used you. Be prepared to hear, "I thought you went out of business." You'll get this response frequently if you haven't contacted them in more than one year. A very small percentage (less than 5 percent) may have moved or died. You'll find out, unfortunately, that many are using another company now. Incentivize them to come back.

Next, look at your advertising activities. Hopefully you have tracked results throughout the year so you know where your leads are coming from. If you haven't, this is your first business-plan goal. Assuming that you have tracked your leads, you know what advertising worked well and what didn't give you the results you expected. Plan to repeat the activities that worked well and determine why the others didn't work well, so that you can either fix the problems or not do them again.

Then look at what you did from a public-relations perspective this year. Public relations includes all non-paid advertising, including donations made to charitable organizations, articles that appeared in the media, etc. Plan on doing more public-relations activities. They usually produce better results than advertising does.

Examine your trade show results. Many times they are difficult to do; mainly because your feet hurt and you have to get people to man the booth for a weekend. However, they are a great source of leads if you are creative in your booth and get people to stop by.

Here are questions to ask when determining your marketing goals:

- How many active customers do you have this year? How many do you want next year?
- How many inactive customers do you have?
- What social media marketing/advertising did you do this year?
- What traditional marketing/advertising activities did you do this year?
- What worked? What didn't work? How do you know?
- What are the marketing plans for next year?
- What public-relations activities did you do this year?
- What public-relations activities are planned for next year?

A simple spreadsheet is all you need for determining and tracking your marketing activities. Your plan is a single sheet of paper. The entire year's activities are shown. The activities are broken down by week. The beauty is that you can look at this sheet of paper every day, every week, or at a minimum, every month when you receive your financial statements. It should be posted on the wall as a reminder of what you need to do and the results of the efforts you've made.

The marketing activity sheet is created by putting *all* of the activities that you will do for the year along the y-axis and the months of the year along the x-axis. Divide the marketing activities into categories: current customers, prospective customers, and employees. Some activities, such as newsletters, you may use for both prospective and current customers.

Figure 21 shows some suggestions for your marketing activities. This is not a complete list of every marketing action you can take. It is simply meant as a guideline to help you plan your activities.

Place an "X" under the week that you plan to do each activity. For public-relations activities or media purchases in radio, television, or newspaper, it is helpful to put the planned action or source's name on the x-axis as a reminder to you. There are some activities, such as telephone follow up and websites, that you will have an "X" under every week. That is okay.

Once the marketing sheet is complete, put it on a wall to remind you of what you have to do each month. Or, if you delegate this responsibility to another employee, it is a quick way of reviewing activities and the results of those activities.

PAGE 3: BUDGET

Your financial statements are your scorecard. Here are some background questions to ask before you begin the financial budget planning process:

- Are you getting your monthly financial statements in a timely manner?

2011 Marketing Flow Chart

Marketing Activity	January			February				March			
	2	9	16	12	30	6	13	20	27	5	12	19	26
Postcards												
Letters												
Newsletters - mail												
Newsletters - Electronic												
Website												
Facebook												
LinkedIn												
Thank you emails												
Referral Program												
Open House												
Yellow Pages												
Radio												
Newspaper												
Television												
Cable												
Billboard												
Trade Journal												
Trade Show												
Public Relations Campaign												

Figure 21. Sample Advertising/Marketing Flow Chart

- Are your financial statements formatted in a manner that helps you with your business?
- Are your financial statements accurate?
- Are you calculating your operational ratios and trailing data each month?
- What are your sales goals?
- What are your gross-margin goals?
- What are your overhead goals?
- What are your net-profit goals?

When you create your budget for the upcoming year, look at what happened this year. Did you have revenues or lack of revenues because of situations out of your control (i.e., the economy, the weather, a competitor going bankrupt, one of your top employees going into business and taking your customers, etc.) or did you do some creative referral/marketing programs to generate new customers that caused sales to increase? This year's results should be the basis for next year's budget.

Look at what happened during the year and make reasonable assumptions about what you will accomplish next year. Then, when you begin the new year, make a final goal to review the financial statements every month with respect to the budget you created. This way you can tell whether you are on track or need to adjust the budget.

IMPLEMENTING THE THREE PAGES

- Decide what to share.
- Put goals where everyone can see them.
- Put marketing/advertising flow chart where everyone can see it.

- Communicate progress towards achieving goals.
- Solicit input.
- Review budget versus actual financial results each month.
- Track results.
- Alter as necessary.

For the first page, your list of goals for the year, remember that the goals must be specific and date oriented so you can measure your progress. "Increase sales" is not a goal. "Increase sales by 25 percent" is. "Increase the sales volume from $500,000 to $1,000,000 by December 31, 20XX" is a better goal.

Put your goals where your employees and you can see them often. This is a consistent, subtle reminder for you to get them accomplished.

Put the second page, your marketing/advertising plan, where your employees can see it often too. They will ask about the results of the specific activities that you plan to do. Make sure you track results so you can share your successes.

You can track results on this grid. Make a copy of the grid and, instead of an "X," put the response percentage. This allows you to easily see which forms of advertising and public relations are effective for you.

For the third page, your financial budget, you probably don't want to put this sheet where everyone can see it. However, you need to keep it where you can compare "budget to actual" results each month when you get your financial statements. An Excel spreadsheet is perfect for doing this. If you create your budget on a spreadsheet, then it is very easy to input the monthly numbers to make sure that you are on track to meet your financial goals.

These three pages help keep you on track. You might ask, "Where are the employee goals?" They are actually accounted for on the sheets. For example, if one of your goals is to hire another employee or manager, you would have this in your goals list and reflect the expenses associated with this (ads, another truck, a salary, increased revenues, etc.) in the financial budget.

Of course, these are summary sheets. Review the goals and marketing plan grid each month when you review your financial statements. List the activities you need to do in the next month to stay on track. Review the activities of the past month. Did you accomplish what you wanted to do? Why or why not?

Have the courage to report results and make changes as necessary to accomplish your goals.

Chapter 17

Conclusions...or Beginnings

"The courage to be profitable" means that you plan your business and work your plan. You measure your progress against budget, and you review accurate financial statements on a monthly basis—calculating the ratios as well as the business trends. This should take no more than thirty minutes each month—a small investment in profitability.

I'll end this book the way I started it—with the story of two companies.

> *Charlie and Sam each own a business in a different metropolitan area. They are in the same industry and approximately the same size. Both companies have ten great, profitable years. Charlie saved the cash from the profits and resists the temptation to spend the vast amount of cash the company accumulated in ten years. He kept the*

140

company's expenses low, even though there was the cash t o spend.

Sam did not resist the temptation to spend all of the cash. He bought vacation homes, boats, expensive travel, and more. The retained earnings of the company never increased. All of the profits were bonused out to owners.

The economy crashed. The market in both geographic areas shrank significantly. Charlie had the cash to weather the downturn. Sam went out of business because the company didn't have the cash to weather the downturn.

Once you are profitable, and sustain profitability, have the courage to say "no" to extravagant spending.

Have the courage to be profitable—in the present and in the future. When you spot issues that are not trending the right way, don't hide them. Have the courage to fix the problems. Your company's survival depends on it.

Acknowledgments

A VERY SPECIAL THANK YOU goes to my clients over the past thirty-one years. Without you, I never would have discovered my ability to teach the financial part of business in English rather than accounting babble.

Next, I would like to thank Brenda Bethea, my assistant for more than twenty years. She has watched the growth, the failures, the near misses, and the successes over the years.

I would be remiss if I didn't thank my parents for their love and support over the years. Even though my father is now in another dimension, I still hear his voice in the back of my head. My father taught me that when bad things happen, you pick yourself up, dust yourself off, and keep going. I did it, Daddy, despite how hard it was at times. And to my mother, who was there to lend an ear and give me a hug whenever I needed it. You both always supported my various endeavors, even when you thought I was nuts. Thank you.

To my daughter Kate, who told me when she was thirteen that she never would own a business. You started yours as soon as you graduated from college. I know that you have implemented what your mother taught you, and you will continue to have a profitable business!

Last but not least, to my husband, Bob. Even though I don't always say it and I don't always show it, a million thank yous are not enough. The journey we're traveling together hasn't always been fun. But it's never been dull. Without you, I wouldn't have gotten through the tough years. At times, you believed in me more than I believed in myself. So this time I'm saying it in print—*thank you.*

About the Author

RUTH KING is a seasoned entrepreneur. Over the past 30+ years, she has owned seven businesses. Her first business, Business Ventures Corporation, began operations in 1981. Through Business Ventures Corporation, she coaches, trains, and helps businesses achieve the business goals they want to achieve. She also started and currently operates Ribbon, The Internet Broadcasting Network and its channels, HVACChannel.tv, ProfitabilityChannel.com, DivaoftheDollars.com, and TurnOnMyFinancialLightBulb.com.

She is especially proud of one company she helped climb out of a big hole. The owner started with a negative $400,000 net worth fifteen years ago and is still in business today—profitably and with a positive net worth.

Ruth started a branch of the Small Business Development Center in Decatur, Georgia in 1982. She also started the Women's

Entrepreneurial Center and taught a year-long course for women who wanted to start their own businesses. This course was the foundation for one of the classes at the Women's Economic Development Authority in Atlanta, Georgia.

More recently Ruth was the instructor for ICE, the Inner City Entrepreneur program, in conjunction with the Small Business Administration. This sixteen-week course taught business owners with at least $400,000 in revenues (and many had over $1,000,000 in revenues) how to grow to the next level. A large part of the curriculum was aimed at improving the financial knowledge of the business owners enrolled in the course.

Ruth holds an MBA in finance from Georgia State University. She also holds bachelor's and master's degrees in chemical engineering from Tufts University and the University of Pennsylvania, respectively.

Ruth is passionate about helping adults learn to read, photography, and marathon races. She helped start an adult literacy organization in 1986 that currently serves over 1,000 adults per year, and she has run ten marathons, including the Boston Marathon.

She was the 2006 USA Best Books Winner for Entrepreneurship and a finalist for the Independent Publisher Awards (IPPY) for her first book, *The Ugly Truth about Small Business* (Sourcebooks). Her second book, *The Ugly Truth about Managing People*, was published by Sourcebooks in 2007.

Ruth is a down-to-earth, thought-provoking speaker and trainer who provides audiences with ideas that inspire them and help them earn more profits. Contact Ruth at rking@ontheribbon.com.

Note: If you would like the templates for all of the forms and graphs in *The Courage to Be Profitable*, go to www.thecouragetobeprofitable.com/downloads.